What All Spirit Babies Want Their Mamas to Know

Otherworldly Wisdom to Support the Journey to Motherhood and the Journey to Awakening

Kate Street

Copyright © 2017 Kate Street
All rights reserved.

ISBN: 1543289371
ISBN 13: 9781543289374

*Loving shout-outs to Elisabeth Hallett, the pioneer of prebirth communication,
To Elizabeth Carman and Neil Carman for their important work in the other realms,
And to Walter Makichen, who coined the phrase "spirit babies."*

Contents

	Introduction	ix
	Part One	1
1	**Introduction to the Spirit Baby Realm**	3
	Do I Have a Spirit Baby?	3
	The Work of Our Generation	4
	The Spirit Baby Realm	7
	My First Experience of Prebirth Communication	7
2	**Spirit Baby Basics**	11
	A Word About Timelines and Intuitives	11
	A Word About Outcomes	12
	Choosing Our Families	13
3	**Prebirth Communication**	15
	Prebirth Communication as Consciousness Expansion	15
	Is This Prebirth Communication?	16
	Strengthening Prebirth Communication	17
	Dreams	18
	Signs	18
	Totems	20
	Journaling	21
	Meditation	21
	Summing Up	22
	Don't Forget the Fathers!	22
	Adoption and Prebirth Communication	23

4	**Challenges On The Way To Mothering**	24
	Trying to Conceive	26
	Miscarriage	28
	Stillbirth	31
	Pregnancy After a Loss	32
	Abortion	34
	We Don't Have to "Earn" Our Babies	39
	Healing a Traumatic Birth Experience	40
5	**Spirit Baby Wisdom on Pregnancy and Birth**	44
	The Best Pregnancy Advice Ever	44
	Getting Ready for Your Empowered Birth	47
6	**When We Get Prebirth Communication "Wrong"**	53
	When Getting It "Wrong" is the Highest Path	54

Part Two — 61

7	**Your Vibrational Journey**	63
	Awakening to LOVE	64
	What Limitlessness Looks Like	64
	Frequency Jumping	68
	It's Really About Self-Love	73
8	**Physical Considerations**	74
	Pain	75
	Fatigue and Exhaustion	76
	Weight Gain	76
	Food Matters, Until It Doesn't	79
9	**Dark Night of the Soul**	81
10	**Working With The New Energy**	85
	The Magic of a Limitless Life	87
	How it Feels	87
	How It Looks	89
	Limitless Pregnancy and Birth	90
	Am I Bat-Shit Crazy?	90
	We Don't Have to Wait	93

Part Three	95
11 Your Spirit Baby Reading	97
FAQ's	105
About the Author	111
Thank You	112
Additional Resources from Kate Street and Love From Baby	114

Introduction

About This Book

Welcome to the Spirit Baby Realm, Dear Sister! It's going to be quite the journey we take together. My hope is that this book will lift you up, expand your perception, and help you see with new eyes as you open up to the wisdom of your spirit baby and of your own limitlessness.

The first thing you should know is that prebirth communication is not a gift. It's an ability we all have. In fact if you're holding this book in your hands, it's already happening to you. Make no mistake that your baby led you to this book, all for the express purpose of talking to you.

Reading this book will give you direct access to your spirit baby and increase your own prebirth communication ability exponentially.

However, Dear Sister, this is so much more than a book about prebirth communication and spirit babies. It's about the awakening in global consciousness that is occurring right now. A new world is being birthed and it looks very different than the world we've been living in. This new world is one of limitlessness, fearlessness, amazing creativity, joy, and play. At the foundation of this world is unconditional love. The babies coming in right now carry within them the frequency of the new world. If you are reading these words, it is an invitation from your spirit baby to join him or her in that frequency.

The words within this book will activate you as they trigger your remembering ~ the remembering of your true nature, which is so much more expansive than you've ever imagined.

A lot of people talk of the awakening consciousness as enlightenment or ascension. I call it LIMITLESSNESS. I experienced an initiation years ago where I discovered how it felt to be wholly integrated ~ the human and divine reunited and working as one. I can only describe it as joyful, fearless, LIMITLESSNESS. It was an amazing feeling (big, contented sigh) and I've been chasing it ever since. I'm stepping into that vibration more and more every day, as we all are.

This book is not timeless. It has a shelf-life. The ideas presented, that at times will seem "impossible" now, will be self-evident in just a few years. We are all transitioning from an old world based on fear to a new world based on love. It's an entirely different level of experience. This book is an aid during the transition.

This book is also a paradigm shift and a portal to the new world, but most of all it's a book about LOVE. A LOVE we have never experienced on this Earth, nor within ourselves, until now. Although we'll talk of the spirit baby realm at length, this book is really about YOU, Dear Sister, and your journey of transformation. Come join me and your baby in the new world.

About You

I already know some things about you. If you're interested in this book it means that you have a very special role as parent of the new world. I know that your children are (and will be) amazing beings who carry a very high vibration. I know that at your core you are a big, bright shining light with many amazing and awe-inspiring gifts. Some of those gifts will emerge as you go along the path of rediscovering your true self.

WHAT ALL SPIRIT BABIES WANT THEIR MAMAS TO KNOW

I also know that you are at the end of a journey and the beginning of another one. Your journey in learning through suffering and pain is coming to an end. All those painful experiences served their higher purpose and you needed to have them as part of your soul's evolution, but you don't have to learn through pain any longer.

You are now starting a journey into the universe of yourself, where you'll discover your brightest light and your deepest love. If you've already been on a path of self-discovery you'll notice it accelerate within these pages. I often repeat important key concepts throughout the book ~ this is to activate and anchor the NEW within you.

This is a time of new beginnings, new discoveries, and experiencing yourself in a new way ~ a way that changes everything around you for the better and for good.

About Me

I'm just like you. I'm a spirit baby intuitive and I've had some amazing spiritual experiences, but I've had my share of difficulties and challenges as well. On the way to mothering my three boys, I experienced two miscarriages and went through a difficult period of trying to conceive. Even though I didn't know it back then, those experiences were key in helping me become who I am today. I wouldn't be able to understand the spirit baby realm as comprehensively as I do today without those past experiences of difficulty (no matter how much they sucked at the time).

I'm also a forerunner, meaning I started my expansion into higher consciousness a bit sooner than most. I have a far-reaching view, which means I can see future timelines well before they become a reality. This is blessing because I can see how GOOD things are going to get. It's also a curse because well, hurry up already! When you can see how GOOD it can be, you just want it that way now!

On my spiritual journey I experienced a three year period of the "dark night of the soul" where I had to wrestle all my dragons. Repeatedly. Like over and over and over. Ad nauseum. The good news for you is that no one will suffer the darkness as long as the forerunners. We had to pave a path where there wasn't one before. The people awakening behind us will awaken much faster and easier. And no....that is not a note of jealousy you detect....anyway, I digress.

Like you, I've evolved through suffering. Like you, that time is over for me.

Now I experience myself in an effortless flow (most of the time anyway). I understand the true nature of my being and realize the value in all my emotions. I trust my inner heart more than anything else. I've expanded way beyond my previous self and feel life to be a joyful divine orchestra. That doesn't mean that things are always great or the way I'd prefer all the time or that shit never happens. It means I can see the perfection in all things just the way they are. I'm content amidst my transformation. That is TRUE FREEDOM.

I write like I speak, so you'll notice many words throughout this book stressed with CAPITAL letters and some important sentences **bolded**. I tried refraining from this, but it felt inauthentic. I'm expressive when I talk and expressive when I write, even if the grammar police don't like it.

Part One

1

Introduction to the Spirit Baby Realm

Do I Have a Spirit Baby?

That's a question I get a lot. And the answer is very simple. If you want to be a mother, then yes, you have a spirit baby. The desire for a baby is never a one-way street. **If a woman yearns for a baby, that baby also yearns for the mother.**

The yearning for a baby is also the ability to feel the energy of your baby around you. You don't have to be pregnant to have a spirit baby around you. In fact, more and more spirit babies are making contact well before conception because some preparation may have to be done before the baby is ready to come in. Often times the mother starts to feel the yearning for a baby more palpably as the time for the spirit baby to come in draws closer. If you're holding this book in your hands, then you have a spirit baby who wants to communicate with you. It also means there might be some work to do.

The Work of Our Generation

With each generation there is a stair-step jump in consciousness and frequency. Our parents are on a stair-step higher than our grandparents and we're on a stair-step higher than our parents. The children coming in now, however, are not merely a stair-step above us ~ they're up a whole gigantic quantum leap! What does that mean? It means the children coming in now will bring with them a clearer remembrance of HOME. They'll bring more limitlessness and fearlessness. They'll have a certainty of the roles they came to play in this lifetime. Most of all, they'll carry within them the frequency of unconditional love at all times.

All babies from all generations come in with the vibration of unconditional love (as that is the true frequency that we all vibrate to and reside in when we're not here on Earth), but due to the condition of the world up until now, that unconditional love vibration was stamped out of us through the social conditioning of parents, teachers, authority figures, peers and society at large. There's no judgment about this and no one to blame ~ this lower vibrating world was an experiment we all agreed to experience for the purpose of our souls' evolution. **But the time of squashing our natural state is over.**

More-over, the children coming in won't stand for it. These high-vibrating children are quite self-possessed, meaning they KNOW who they are. If we're having dark moments of feeling limited or fearful, and then attempting to impose those limits and fears on them, they'll know it's all about us and not about them. That's great news in that the fear of parents "ruining" kids does not apply anymore. We CAN'T ruin them, they're too rooted in the truth of who they are. However, it also means that they'll do their best to blast our limits to the ground, using whatever means necessary. They'll test us and push our buttons over and over until we start to see things in expanded ways. Many of the battles you see today in the growing generation is the result of higher vibrating children doing their best to break through the limits of their parents and society at large. It can be quite contentious raising a high-vibrating soul if the parent is stuck in a lower vibration, unwilling to relent.

Thankfully, that won't be YOUR experience, Dear Sister. Even though you already vibrate at a high frequency (or you wouldn't be reading these words in the first place), the invitation from your spirit baby is to make that quantum leap into unconditional love with him or her. When we can meet our children where they are, we can parent in a different way ~ a JOYFUL way. Our role will be less authoritative and more partnership. We will be able see our children for the BIG souls they are and honor their inherent interests, passions, and desires without trying to make them fit into a box that no longer fits even us. Instead of constantly worrying about our children, we can explore new territory with them. A new world of parenting is truly available now!

Which is why some work needs to be done first.

I often say in my blog posts and in my spirit baby readings that our generation has it toughest in this whole "global-transforming-consciousness" thingy that's occurring right now. We have the dual role of REMEMBERING our true nature of LIMITLESSNESS and FEARLESSNESS while forgetting EVERYTHING we've been taught up until now. And I do mean everything. Well, at least everything we've been taught that tells us we're not enough, that we should be afraid, that we're limited, that the world is scary, that we need things outside of ourselves to be whole. So yeah, everything.

The world up until now has been one based on fear and lack. And it's a lie.

The children coming in know the truth and won't believe the lies. It's time to stop believing the lies and to stop telling the lies ~ especially to ourselves.

When we can step into our own limitlessness and fearlessness, we can recognize and honor the limitlessness and fearlessness in others, especially our children. **It's from our own limitlessness that we will create the new world WITH our children.**

Luckily, expanding into our limitlessness is an organic, natural process. It's nothing we have to force as it's already happening ~ sort of like a time-release-capsule from our soul. It isn't always pretty and it's certainly not always easy, but we're never given more than we can handle. Any difficulties along the way are coming up for final observation and release. The keys to not suffering through transformation are NON-RESISTANCE and SELF-LOVE.

Dear Sister, you're about to either start your transformation or accelerate it. All those things that you've allowed to scare you or limit you will come up for you to look at and this time you can make a new choice. You're switching from fear to love, from "everything is scary" to "anything is possible." And there are some dragons along the way.

But I'll tell you a secret about dragons, if you can love them instead of fear them, they'll turn from fearsome creatures to adoring companions. When in doubt, LOVE THE DRAGON.

So, do you have to have your vibration at a certain frequency before your spirit baby will come to you? Absolutely not. The journey of evolution is never ending, there is no finish line. You don't have to "earn" your spirit baby and you don't even have to raise your vibration to welcome him or her in. You're raising your vibration because it's something you planned to do before coming into this lifetime. It's the reason FOR this lifetime. Everyone, at some point, will be going through a transformation of consciousness and they'll use various avenues and have various guides to get there.

You're choosing now. And your spirit baby is helping you.

WHAT ALL SPIRIT BABIES WANT THEIR MAMAS TO KNOW

The Spirit Baby Realm

As you read along you'll notice that the spirit baby realm is one of profound love. There is no judgment nor regret in the spirit baby realm, only expansive acceptance and understanding.

The spirit baby realm is part of The Other Side where souls go when they die. We've known for a while that we can contact people who've passed away. Finally it's becoming common knowledge that we can also connect to souls who are planning on coming in. The spirit baby realm is a special place on the Other Side where souls are planning their next incarnation on Earth. I've found it's easier (and preferable for all involved) to think of them as spirit babies, rather than souls. It helps prepare both the parents and the children for the respective roles they'll be playing.

However, while we can and should think of these souls as babies, we need to also understand they have the higher perspective and can guide us while they are on the Other Side. They understand the vibrational leap we are taking as a generation and want to help in any way they can. Any change to a higher frequency helps us and in turn, helps them. You can say your spirit baby has a vested interest in your transformation. Often they act as catalysts to their parents' spiritual transformation (which I'll talk about later).

The babies coming in now REALLY want to talk to their parents. Prebirth communication is becoming more recognized as more people experience it. And more people are experiencing it because the babies are initiating it. Which brings us to...

My First Experience of Prebirth Communication

I'd just had a devastating miscarriage. At a week 12 ultrasound my husband and I discovered that our baby did not have a heartbeat and had, in fact, stopped growing around week 8. After hearing our options, I decided to miscarriage naturally rather than have a hospital procedure. My husband and I went home to quietly grieve.

In my time of mourning my midwife suggested I do a meditation where I could meet my baby in a safe place and we could exchange gifts and say goodbye. I'd never been a great meditator, but decided I would try it just for the sake of closure. I have to admit I sort of half-assed the meditation, not being able to concentrate fully. However, I was faintly able to envision meeting my baby boy on a beach where I gifted him with a seashell and he gifted me back a green piece of sea-glass. I finished the meditation with a few tears and then went on about my day, not giving it another thought.

Until a few days later, when my world was rocked.

I was visiting my friend, Sheila, who'd just returned from vacation in Florida. Sheila had brought a gift for me and I was sitting on her couch opening it. When I saw what it was, I had what I can only describe as a "soul reaction." Before I even understood what was happening, my soul told me "Sit up! Pay attention! Something important is happening!"

After a moment of cognitive dissonance, I finally understood what I was looking at: a necklace with a green piece of seaglass.

My body got covered with chills. I KNEW this was a sign from my baby.

I told Sheila the story of my meditation and she said, "You know, it's so funny. I saw that necklace and just knew it was yours. I've never seen you wear silver and almost didn't get it, but I knew you had to have that necklace."

We both knew it was my spirit baby working through her.

Now a funny thing about this story, there was a also a little silver sea turtle pendant along with the sea glass. I remember thinking at the time, "If only it was just the sea glass it'd be perfect. What do I need with a turtle?" I tried taking the turtle pendant off the necklace but it refused to budge no matter what I did. I thought that was strange. Why couldn't I remove this tiny turtle pendant?

It wasn't until a week later when another friend of mine, Kimberly, heard my story as I showed her my necklace that I understood why the turtle refused to be removed. Kimberly said "You know that turtles represent Motherhood, right?"

Mind blown.

Along with the green sea glass representing our good-bye, my baby gave me an even bigger gift ~ a turtle representing Motherhood. **I knew in that moment that my baby was promising he would come back.**

While that green piece of sea-glass comforted me and showed me the proof of communication with my spirit baby, that little silver turtle gave me the promise of our future. It also taught me not to discard things I don't understand, for in them may contain bigger gifts.

I've learned this repeatedly in the readings I give. Often times I'm tempted to discard a piece of information because it seems strange or I don't understand it or it just feels plain weird relaying it. Well, let me tell you, every time I relay that strange piece of information is when something magical happens. It's when something clicks into place for the other person. It doesn't matter if I understand it, it only matters if the person the message is meant for understands it. If Sheila had listened to the part of herself that knew I didn't wear silver, I may have missed out on a great message. I've come to relish the strange information I don't immediately understand, as I know it's taking me on some new adventure.

That turtle was also my first animal totem. A totem is a natural object or animal believed to have spiritual significance. Spirit babies are BIG on totems and gifts of all kinds (which I'll mention in its own section later). So if one shows up in your life, even when you don't understand it, listen to your soul who is undoubtably saying "Sit up! Pay attention! Something important is happening!"

2

Spirit Baby Basics

<u>A Word About Timelines and Intuitives</u>

There are infinite timelines and infinite possibilities to choose from, Dear Sister. With each decision and reaction we choose the timeline we're going to interact with and experience. I'm not going to boggle my own mind by trying to explain it, nor do I think I could. The only thing we need to understand is that **if we don't like the timeline we're experiencing, we have the power within us to change it.** Sometimes it's a small action that can change timelines. Sometimes it's an intention or affirmation. Sometimes it's an invitation from a spirit baby.

Because there are infinite timelines to choose from, getting an intuitive reading can sometimes be tricky. The intuitive or psychic does a reading not only from the timeline that you are resonating with, but also from the timeline *they* are resonating with. If you are vibrating at a higher frequency than the intuitive, then she (or he) may not even be able to see the higher timelines that are available to you from her (or his) vantage point. I stopped seeking intuitive readings outside myself years ago when I noticed my vision had become father reaching than theirs. Don't let anyone impose limitations on you, not even a psychic or intuitive.

I would describe myself as a "best-case-scenario" intuitive. I don't pretend to know all the timelines or possibilities, but I can see and feel into ones that are infinitely better than what we're experiencing now. And because I choose to align with that particular vision, I start to vibrate to the frequency of that vision, thereby bringing it into reality (even if it takes much longer than I'd like, dammit).

When I do an intuitive reading, I'm presenting a woman with her best-case-scenario from the spirit baby's perspective. The spirit baby is all seeing and knows the highest experiences his mama has chosen for herself. The reading is an invitation (and an activation) from the baby for the mama to now step into that very high-vibrating timeline.

If you find yourself resonating with a certain concept while reading this book, and it triggers a remembering of your soul's purpose, **then simply intend to align with it.** At any time and in any situation you can always just intend to "align with the highest possible outcome for all involved," and that will put you on the best-case-scenario timeline.

A Word About Outcomes

However, all that being said, while we CAN align with the highest timelines, that doesn't necessarily mean we get to choose the outcome. Letting go of expectations and outcomes is a large part of the work in dragon fighting (some call it "shadow work").

When aligning with the highest timelines, don't focus on specifics or details. **Often times expectations limit the outcomes available to us.** If we let go of our attachment to outcomes, we free up a whole lot of energy, so that what we're presented with is so much better than what we previously imagined.

Align with the best-case-scenarios without deciding what it should be in advance. Just that alone is a huge turn-key to freedom and limitlessness.

<u>Choosing Our Families</u>
Yes, it's true. We all choose our parents. I know some of us don't care to hear that because our families seem crazy or sometimes even cruel. But we choose the people to raise us based on what they will help develop in us. Sometimes the choice is based on karmic reasons. Sometimes we have things to overcome and our families provide the best dragons for us.

Before incarnating to Earth we all write up life contracts and interweave them with all the people we'll interact with in our lifetimes. We draw up different scenarios that best fit the evolution of our soul.

And the truth is, often times the people who treat us the worst are our most loving companions on the Other Side. Who else but someone who deeply loves you and deeply cares about the evolution of your soul would agree to come into this incarnation as an utter bastard just to treat you like shit? I'm joking, but not really.

The point is, we came into this lifetime with baggage, karma, and crap to clean up. We chose the families that would help us do just that.

But that's one more thing that is now changing.

The spirit babies being born now are coming in karma free and without baggage. Which means WE now get to become karma and baggage free too! Can you imagine a world filled with families who don't crap on each other?! Hallelujah, I say!

Now instead of choosing parents based on karma or who will help them clean up their crap, spirit babies are choosing parents based on who will help them keep their high frequency, who will help support their biggest dreams and desires, and who will walk alongside them creating a new world based on unconditional love. Ahhhhh....doesn't that feel better?

"Are all the babies who are coming now in karma-free?" you may be asking. My answer is, "Huh, I don't know." I know other intuitives connect with spirit babies who give very different information than what I receive. I've been shocked while hearing a spirit baby tell another intuitive they were angry at their mother for one reason or another. That is not the kind of information I get. Ever.

I'm not aligned with the babies coming in with karma. I don't get that information because I don't vibrate to it. I'm aligned with the higher vibrating babies who are planning to come in karma-free. And more importantly, SO ARE YOU. You and your baby may have some work to do to clear the karma before he or she comes however, and that's a large part of what this whole book (and your journey) is all about.

Everyone will work through their own stuff in their own time, so don't worry about anyone else. It's all perfectly orchestrated to their own timing.

It's your time NOW to become karma free and to bring in a no-baggage-baby. Rest assured, if you're reading these words, the highest possible scenario is available to you and your spirit baby is helping guide you there.

3

Prebirth Communication

Prebirth Communication as Consciousness Expansion

More and more spirit babies are breaking through the veil to connect to their mamas. This is due to the expansion of consciousness that's happening globally right now and it's also to help it along.

Would-be-mamas are becoming more open and attuned to such communication and in turn, the spirit baby becomes a guide of sorts to help expand his mama's consciousness even more.

Every human has a team of guides that help us along our paths in life. At this time on Earth, many spirit babies are joining that team of guides to connect with their mamas. And it makes sense, as any raise in consciousness will benefit the baby coming in, as well as the mother herself.

However, the spirit baby realm doesn't want all the credit for our raising consciousness. What happens during prebirth communication is that the energy of our spirit baby melds with the energy of our higher selves (the part of us that has the same expanded perception as our spirit babies). The spirit baby energy then acts as an amplifier to our own intuition, thereby bringing to light a bit brighter the things we already know deep in our souls.

I can't even imagine how very different my first birth would have been without the gentle, loving guidance of my spirit baby. Before getting pregnant, my mantra regarding childbirth was "Give me the epidural, I'm nobody's hero!" Suffice to say, the thought of unassisted homebirth, the way I gave birth to all three of my boys, was not even on my radar. It was through prebirth communication that this option entered into my realm of possibilities. Instead of childbirth being something to fear, like we've learned through all sorts of bullshit cultural conditioning, I learned that it can actually be an incredibly empowering and amazing peak experience that is completely life-changing.

When we engage in prebirth communication with our spirit babies, it helps strengthen our intuition and the belief in our inner wisdom as our one true authority. When we're listening so intently within, it becomes easier to tune out the voices around us that attempt to keep us in fear and limitation. This is especially important during pregnancy and birth, when we're surrounded by "experts" whose main focus is on what could go wrong.

Communicating with our spirit babies can help expand us into possibilities we didn't even know existed before. New paths are illuminated, paths that lead us to our own limitlessness and amazing peak experiences.

Is This Prebirth Communication?
Women often write to me with dreams of their babies and wonder if they're having prebirth communication. Or something unusual will happen making them wonder if it's a sign from their spirit baby.

WHAT ALL SPIRIT BABIES WANT THEIR MAMAS TO KNOW

Whenever I get a question from a woman asking if they're experiencing prebirth communication, my answer is always invariably, "Yes!" **If you think you're experiencing prebirth communication, then you're experiencing prebirth communication.** It really is that simple and straightforward. The fact that you're reading this book is a clear indication that you're already in communication with your spirit baby. Women don't need answers as much as they need validation. Many women come to me already knowing the answers they seek, they just need someone to help them trust those answers.

Women have been having prebirth communication even before the term "prebirth communication" was invented. Back then it was simply mother's intuition. When we just KNOW the baby we're pregnant with is a girl, that's prebirth communication. When we just KNOW what the name of our unborn baby is, that's prebirth communication. But it goes so much deeper than that. Our spirit babies can tell us their favorite colors, their personality traits, and foods they'll like when they come Earthside. They can tell us what they look like, what their favorite animals are, and what hobbies they'll like. They can tell us so much about themselves.

They also know so much about us too. And their fathers. And well, just about everything from their birds-eye-view from The Other Side. With prebirth communication, we can get to know the personalities and preferences of our future children but we can also get the benefit of their wisdom. More and more spirit babies are stepping up to the plate to act as guides for their parents during these transitory times. If you're reading these words, this is the case for you. So, since you have a spirit baby so obviously connecting with you, let's do whatever we can to strengthen that communication...

Strengthening Prebirth Communication
The first thing we need to do to strengthen communication is to BELIEVE that we are having it. A simple acknowledgment of "Okay,

baby I know you're communicating with me," and an intention of "I'm open and willing to listen," is a perfect introduction to each other. From there be open to the following methods your spirit baby may be using to send you messages:

Dreams
Dreams are the realm of the spirit babies. It's by far the most common method babies use to alert their mamas of their presence or to send them messages. A large percentage of women are prompted to find me due to dreams their spirit babies sent them. Dreams are the easiest way to get in touch with us because our minds are quiet and they can more effectively get through. Many times the dreams of our spirit babies are very vivid. We may wake up right afterwards to ensure we don't forget them. Two of my boys told me their names through dream messages. Dreamtime is also where I learned their genders and what they looked like. We can get many messages from our babies during dreamtime. If you want to strengthen communication, tell your baby you're open to this and then write down any dream messages you receive. It's a great way to get to know your baby without our pesky minds getting in the way.

Disclaimer: Not all dreams about our babies during pregnancy are messages. When we're pregnant, dreamtime is also a time to work out our fears and worries. Many pregnant woman have nightmares about things happening to their babies. In most cases, this is not prebirth communication. These are not warnings from our babies, but merely our own (very important) process of bringing our fears to the surface for release. Sometimes, in extreme cases, our spirit baby may send us a warning through a dream. If this is the case you'll get further confirmation in other places. My point is don't fear that every scary dream you have means something "bad" is going to happen.

Signs
Signs from your spirit baby can come in many forms too unique and varied to even try to list. Basically if you think it might be a sign from

your baby then just believe it is. After my first miscarriage is when pre-birth communication really kicked in for me. I started getting signs all over the place. And because I needed the signs so much it was easy for me to believe them.

One winter day I walked out my front door and saw a big green leaf in the walkway on top of the snow. Looking around I had no idea where the leaf could have come from since we were surrounded by pine trees. I paused, wondering if it was a sign from my baby. Then I continued walking to my car, telling myself if it was a sign it would still be there when I got home later. When I got home, the leaf was gone.

The next morning I was walking to my car again and I noticed the leaf was back in exactly the same place. It hadn't been there the afternoon before but it was back now. And I knew it was the same leaf as it had a rip on the right side. That time I knew it was a sign from my baby. I brought it inside and put it on my night-stand on top of a book. And that's when I gasped ~ the cover of my book had a picture of a leaf on it, with a rip on the right side. "Thank you, baby," I said with tears in my eyes.

With my second son, I was given an unmistakeable sign to let me know he was okay. It was early in my pregnancy and I'd woken up to a spot of blood. Having had two miscarriages previously, I assumed it must be happening again. As I prepared myself to miscarry my beloved second baby, I opened a book to a random page. My eyes immediately went to a line that said "Hi Mama, it's me! I'm still here!" And he was still there. I didn't miscarry. Thank you, baby.

Another memorable sign I received was when I was pregnant with my third baby. Through a dream my spirit baby told me that horses would be a favorite animal in this upcoming lifetime. Upon awakening I decided my first gift for my baby would be a stuffed horse. The day I bought the horse I was coming out of the store when I was stopped in my tracks at a the sight of a bumper sticker that said, "I love my horse." I knew it was a sign. Thank you, baby.

As you can see, signs can come in many forms. If you see something unusual that is meaningful to you, assume it's a sign from your baby and thank him or her. An acknowledgment of the sign with gratitude will ensure they keep on coming.

Totems
Totems are one of my absolute favorite spirit babies methods of communication. As mentioned before, a totem is a natural object or animal believed to have spiritual significance. I've told you about my turtle totem, signifying motherhood, sent to me by my first son. My second son sent me dragonflies, symbolizing transformation. And my third son sent me dolphins representing playful humor and joy (he laughed like a dolphin for years too).

How do you recognize your totem? It's an animal (or flower or feather or seashell or whatever) that you see in an obvious, meaningful way or on a repeated basis. It doesn't have to be the exact animal (or object), it can be a representation of one.

Once you recognize your totem (and I've yet to meet a spirit baby who doesn't love to give his mama a totem), look up the spiritual meaning of it. Thank your baby for the gift and then see if you can find a representation of it in the form of a crystal, trinket, or statuette. This is your power animal (or object) throughout your time of conception, pregnancy and birth. Whenever you see one, it's your baby saying hi or offering your encouragement.

Sometimes you may even get more than one totem. The secondary totem from my first son was an owl. I was walking in the woods, thinking about the unassisted homebirth I was gearing myself up for. I was concerned about the safety of it when all of a sudden a huge owl swooped down and landed on a branch right in front of me. I was awed. I stopped on the path and owl and I just stared at each other for the longest time. Then when I started walking again, the owl flew from branch to branch following me. I knew something significant was being communicated. When I got home, I looked up the meaning of owl and amongst many of the various meanings, one stood out to me like a neon sign. It said "when an owl is seen or heard near a pregnant woman it means she'll have an easy birth." Just when I was worrying about our birth, my baby sent me reassurance that all would be fine. Owl is still my favorite bird to this day.

A totem is a beautiful gesture from your spirit baby. It is an amazing and significant gift that will stay with you always.

Journaling
Journaling is a great way to have a two-way conversation with your baby. In my readings many spirit babies recommend journaling to their mamas as a way of communication. The process is simple enough ~ get a journal dedicated to prebirth communication, write a question to your baby, and then free write the answers you get, without thinking about it too much. You'll know the message is from your spirit baby if it's from an expansive place of love. If it's limited and fear-based that's your own stuff, but writing it out is a good way to release it, so it's all good. The more you do it, the more you'll get the hang of it, and the easier it will become. It's a great way to strengthen your intuition and your connection.

Meditation
Although my first attempt at meditating with my spirit baby after my miscarriage was half-assed, it was also amazingly successful. From then on I was hooked. Meditation was my preferred method of deliberate communication when pregnant with my first son (with my other two, I already had kids, so who had time to meditate?). I meditated almost every day back then, just so I could commune with my spirit baby. Since

gearing up for my unassisted homebirth was my most pressing concern, that was often the focus of our conversations.

I would light a candle, put on soothing music, and sit cross-legged on my bed for 20 minutes or so, just listening. Often times I would get what I called "hugs" from my baby. I'd get a message and my body would be blanketed with chills in recognition of TRUTH. Pay attention to any sensations or thoughts you get. Notice repeating themes. Write down anything significant that comes through. Like journalling, the more you do it, the easier it becomes.

After my son and I experienced a successful and beautiful birth, I recorded two meditations based on my own: "Messages from the Womb" and "Beautiful Birth." (Sold as set, both are available on lovefrombaby.com)

Summing Up
Spirit babies may use any or all of these methods to communicate with you. There are other methods as well. Some mamas hear the voice of their spirit babies. Some smell unexplained smells (most often a burning scent). And there are probably other methods I've never even heard of.

When it comes to prebirth communication simply acknowledge it, believe it, and encourage it. If it's meaningful to you, it's communication.

Don't Forget the Fathers!
Fathers also experience prebirth communication. My own husband had dreams of all our babies. Women tend to be more intuitive, so the bond to the spirit baby is often stronger with the mother, but prospective papas should not be left out of the equation. One of my fondest memories was when I was very pregnant with our first son. I woke up in the middle of the night and noticed that my husband had his hand on my belly in his sleep. When he woke up he told me he'd been dreaming of our baby.

WHAT ALL SPIRIT BABIES WANT THEIR MAMAS TO KNOW

If we feel inspired, we should share our prebirth communications with our partners. Just the sharing alone can help open them up to connecting with the spirit baby on their own.

Adoption and Prebirth Communication

I'm often asked if prebirth communication can happen in the case of adoption and the answer is a resounding "Yes!" Spirit babies know who their parents are, no matter how they come to them. Adoption is just another path some souls plan in their life charts for the purpose of soul evolution.

A magical thing I've witnessed with a couple of adoption cases, is communication continuing even after the baby has been born but is still separated. Prebirth communication then develops into telepathic communication between the adoptive mother and the baby.

My friend, Kimberly, experienced this very thing. She and her husband had been waiting for years for a daughter from China. Like most things dependent upon divine timing, this was taking far longer than expected. But Kimberly's connection to her future baby was so strong that she received signs from her the whole three years they were waiting. Her future daughter sent her a daisy flower as a totem. Kimberly knew that every time she saw a daisy it was a sign and a promise from her daughter. I was with Kimberly more than once when we would come upon a daisy in the most unlikely places. One time we had just gotten out of her car to hike in the woods when at Kimberly's feet was a small pink baby hat with daisies all over it. We both got chills and knew her daughter was with us.

When Kimberly finally got her daughter's picture in the mail three years later there was an instant soul recognition. From the very beginning they've had an amazing bond. It's been beautiful to witness.

Adoption is in no way a barrier to prebirth communication. It's all the same phone lines to the Other Side.

4

Challenges On The Way To Mothering

Most women who come to me for a reading have not had an easy journey to Motherhood. You don't really seek answers when everything is going smoothly, so the majority of information I get from the spirit baby realm has to do with complications, difficulties, and often times tragedies.

Spirit babies have a lot to say when it comes to difficulties conceiving, miscarriages, stillbirths and even abortions. Even though all these experiences seem different on the surface, there are common themes among them.

For example all scenarios listed above involve karmic clearing from this lifetime and past lifetimes to different degrees. "But Kate!" I can hear you saying, "You just said that we are becoming karma free!" That's absolutely right, Dear Sister, we are. But as we transition from the old world to the new one, some house-cleaning has to be done. Even many of the babies coming in baggage free first have some clearing to do before

WHAT ALL SPIRIT BABIES WANT THEIR MAMAS TO KNOW

they can come in with a brand-new-shiny-blank-slate. In almost all of the readings I do, there is a partnership between baby and parents to use experiences such as miscarriage or difficulty conceiving as joint karmic clearing for all parties involved.

The spirit babies want to make it clear however, that just because karmic clearing is a huge common theme in all these experiences, this doesn't mean that women who are having difficulties on the path to motherhood have more karma to clear than others. Absolutely not. All humans on Earth right now have their own share of karmic crap to clear and everyone chooses their own unique path to get it done. The mother who gets pregnant easily and repeatedly and has wonderful births will be working on her karmic clearing in other areas.

The spirit babies stress that there shouldn't be judgment around difficulties conceiving or challenges keeping a pregnancy. No one is doing better than anyone else. No one has it all figured out. Everyone has their own crap to deal with and their own dragons to fight in their own unique ways. Period.

And now allow me to let you in on a little secret: once you understand the higher purposes behind all these challenges....you don't have to experience them anymore. And if you've never experienced them, you don't have to be afraid of experiencing them. Someone reading these words has no cause to think "I haven't had any difficulties yet, I wonder if I will because I have karma to clear?" If you're reading this book, chances are you've already worked out a huge chunk of your karma and have surmounted your largest challenges. That's how it works ~ you do your work THEN you get the expanded view. I guess the expanded view during the experience would dampen the impact? Hell, I have no idea why it works like it does. All I know is that I'm supposed to tell you why things have happened, I'm not reporting things that will happen. This truly can be the END of the difficulties. Speaking of which...

Another common theme involved in all the previously mentioned baby-challenged scenarios is suffering. Whether you've been trying to conceive for three years or just had a miscarriage or stillbirth, suffering is a present and persistent companion. **More than anything, spirit babies want to alleviate their mothers' suffering.** They can see the expanded view of all situations, and while they understand that grieving may be necessary, suffering does not have to be.

Let's explore these areas a little more...

Trying to Conceive
Oh, how I remember the period of my life when I was trying to conceive. When I think back to that time so many years ago, the feelings that stand out for me are ones of frustration, impatience, and wild desperation. Sure, there were feelings of hope and promise mingled in, especially during ovulation, but mostly I was a possessed-obsessed-control-freak and NOT much fun to be around. I was known to coerce my husband into having sex when he didn't want to, flip off every pregnant woman around me (behind their backs, of course), and throw HUGE tantrums when my period would arrive. Yes, I was a fucking maniac.

It took my second miscarriage to snap me out of it. By then I was so devastated, so disheartened, and so pissed off that I just chucked my thermometer and my fertility charts into the garbage in a fit of rage. Two months later I got pregnant again, and this time for keeps. It had taken another tragedy for me to finally surrender and let go.

Now granted, not every woman who is trying to conceive is a maniac like I was, but the feelings involved are still the same. There are different degrees of frustration, impatience, pre-occupation, distraction, disappointment, unmet expectations and some definite control issues. **These are the dragons we are fighting when we are stuck in the loop of trying to conceive.** It's all appropriate and exactly as it should be.

WHAT ALL SPIRIT BABIES WANT THEIR MAMAS TO KNOW

And our spirit babies are in on it. They know that "difficulties getting pregnant" is written in our life chart, and they understand their part in all of it. So while we are able to feel our spirit babies, and even communicate with them, they know they have to stay back a bit to let us cleanse, purify, and work through our stuff. Instead of looking at this as a bad thing, we need to understand that we are actually making great leaps and bounds in our spiritual evolution. We are clearing lifetimes worth of shit in just a relatively short amount of time. Truthfully, we are freakin' amazing!

And while it is a journey that is beyond frustrating, if you have been futilely trying to conceive, know that this part of your journey is now over. This is an invitation from your spirit baby to leave that part behind and begin a new path. The cleansing and the purifying is now done. You can finally get out of the loop of frustration.

Know that your spirit baby is close. Know that your spirit baby IS going to come. Leave the timing of it all up to your spirit baby and your soul. **Delays are actually protection ~ protection against getting anything less than your highest desires.** You've put in the work, you've been fighting your dragons, you've cleared so much energy, and you've been raising your vibration as you go (even if it doesn't feel like it). Now is the time to TRUST in your spirit baby and start a new expression of yourself.

We've all heard the advice "just relax and forget about it and you'll get pregnant," and we've all wanted to smack those advice-givers right upside the head. But there is truth in that usually ill-timed, unsolicited advice. It's not about forgetting about it, though. It's about trusting that you deserve your desires and trusting that the baby you feel so strongly around you will come in when the timing is right for his or her incarnation.

MANY spirit babies tell me during readings that they have to wait until the energy on Earth is at a certain frequency to be able to support their very high vibration. Remember, there is a HUGE leap in frequency with these children coming in right now. If the vibration on Earth is not resonant, the babies will wait until there is a raise in frequency, rather than lower theirs. Why come in at a lower frequency when you can just wait a bit so you can be the highest expression of yourself? This is a very common occurrence right now during the transitory period. If these words resonate with you, then they're meant for you. You've done all the work, Dear Sister. Your very high vibrational baby just needs to wait until the Earth can support his or her frequency. And with the global awakening accelerating at such a rapid pace, the wait shouldn't be too much longer.

So trust in all of this and in the meantime, explore a new expression of yourself. Not to "earn" your baby, but to experience yourself in new ways. When we try new things, we create new pathways that help bring in the new energy. All of this will raise our vibration. For ideas on how to do just that, read the section "Frequency Jumping."

The frustrating part of your journey is over, Sister. Know it. You've done it. Your baby is coming to you. Now start something NEW.

Miscarriage

Let's be frank: miscarriages suck. It's a time of lost dreams, secret grief, confusion and guilt. Every one of us who suffers a loss questions, at least for a moment, if it was due to something we did or didn't do. Most of us have already formed a bond and an internal relationship with the baby. Indeed a miscarriage feels like we are losing a most sacred and beautiful part of ourselves. We have to readjust our minds around the due dates and the dreams. And often we're stuck with a body that still feels slightly pregnant, so we can't even easily erase the evidence of our loss. There's nothing easy about miscarriages.

There are a few important things the spirit baby realm wants us to know from their higher perspective about miscarriage to help ease any suffering, so read the following words carefully and take them deep within your heart...

In almost all cases of miscarriage the soul that we lost WILL COME BACK TO US in a subsequent pregnancy. Of course it's up to us to create the circumstances for that pregnancy, but if we are willing to try again, that spirit baby that we already bonded with WILL COME BACK. I felt this so strongly when I was pregnant with my first son. With each miscarriage and the pregnancy that finally stuck, it was so obvious to me that the soul of my baby was the same energy each time. When he was younger my son would sometimes talk about the reasons he left and then came back ~ details to work out, adjustments to make, certain things he had to wait for. I don't think I've ever done a reading for a mama who's miscarried where the baby didn't plan on returning. Dear Sister, **we can and will meet our lost babies again.** Know this and let it bring you comfort.

Similar to the challenges mentioned in the "Trying To Conceive" section, the experience of miscarriage is something we've chosen to experience with our babies, and our partners, for the reasons of soul evolution for all involved. When we experience a loss, it's a catalyst for change. It helps us see what we really want and allows us to put our priorities in order. It's also a heart-opener. It opens us up so deeply in ways we can't even imagine. When we're broken so wide open, it's an opportunity for our world to be re-arranged in new ways that serve our highest purpose.

With miscarriages, there's also karmic clearing going on for both the parents and the baby. The agreement is that the baby will come in for a short amount of time to work in partnership with the parents to clear karma. And usually the karma is from past lives. This doesn't mean we did something "wrong" in a past-life and are now being "punished" for it. It means we're working through old issues for the purpose of our highest soul intentions in this lifetime. Now, that doesn't mean our spirit babies want us to go delving into past lives to find out what those issues are. Quite the opposite. The spirit babies ask us to leave the past in the past, know it's being worked out even if we don't understand it, and to instead look to the new beginnings.

As with everything in our lives, miscarriages have been divinely orchestrated by our souls and our spirit babies, to help us spiritually fast-track our evolution. Miscarriage can be a huge opportunity for growth if we can understand the bigger picture and know that it's leading us to something better.

When our babies come back the next time they'll come in with a higher vibration. The karmic clearing of the miscarriage afforded them this opportunity. Indeed many spirit babies use miscarriage as a vehicle for karmic clearing, as it serves both them and the parents. Karmic clearing will continue to happen as our old worlds are being broken down, making space for new opportunities. I've had so many spirit babies THANK their mamas for giving them the gift of being able to come in as a higher vibrational soul by agreeing to experience the miscarriage. There are many gifts and many opportunities available behind the scenes.

This doesn't mean we shouldn't grieve our miscarriages. Grieving is absolutely appropriate and something we need to allow ourselves to experience fully. Staying stuck in our grief, however, can lead to suffering. And our spirit babies truly want to alleviate any suffering, as it's not necessary. When we believe something went "wrong," or we're being "punished" or we don't "deserve" our babies, that's when suffering ensues. And none of it is true.

We deserve our babies, simply because we desire them. They love us very much, they are working in partnership with us, and they WILL come back. In the meantime, they are still close to us and can communicate with us. Often times, as in my case, miscarriage is what instigates prebirth communication. The yearning for the baby is stronger than ever, making connection almost inevitable. So listen closely for the whispers of your baby. He or she is right there next to you and planning their next incarnation.

Stillbirth

Stillbirth is a heavy, tragic experience to go through. It truly is a life-changing event. Only the strongest of souls agree to come here to experience such a tragedy as losing a baby at birth. And while we must bear the pain of our loss, it's also important that we don't let the loss define us for the rest of our lives. While there is little comfort to be found while experiencing the loss of a stillborn baby, an expanded view (in time) can often help lessen the unrelenting heaviness.

Everything I said in the miscarriage section also applies to stillbirth. It's a divinely orchestrated agreement between parents and babies to experience the tragedy of stillbirth for reasons of spiritual catalysts, heart-openers, soul expansion, vibrational jumping, and karmic clearing. With stillbirth readings, however, I've found there is often more karma that the baby has to work out. They have to stick around for a while longer than babies do in miscarriage as part of the agreement.

One particular reading really stands out for me. A woman came to me because her baby was born still at 36 weeks. She was heartbroken, guilt-ridden, and wanted to know if there was something she should have done differently or better that would have made him stay.

Her sweet baby boy came in right away assuring his mama that all guilt and responsibility for all parties involved should be absolved as nothing was done "wrong." In fact, he told her, this was the highest outcome possible and everything happened just like they'd planned. This baby wanted to come in as one of the new children ~ one without karma and baggage free. But he couldn't do that without first going through this 36 week pregnancy with his parents.

And even though it was a very difficult situation for his parents to currently deal with, he said that had he been born into this existence with this particular pregnancy it would have been a lesser existence for all of them. He said there would have been a more difficult cross to bear in the future for all of them.

He also went on to say that the outcome of this experience had been so successful that not only had it cleared the karma of the parents and the baby, it also cleared the karma for future children. What happened was thorough and EPIC.

This baby was incredibly grateful to his parents for agreeing to this experience, conveying that it was a tremendous gift for all of them. Not only could he come in a higher version of himself, they were now going through vibrational upgrades that would allow them to become the higher versions of themselves. It would be a much more joyful existence for all of them because they went through this experience together.

Now, like miscarriages, of course we need to grieve stillbirths. The grief around stillbirth is denser and must be honored. But again, we can't allow ourselves to be stuck there. Our babies encourage us to grieve the endings fully and then join them in celebrating the bright future we are all now afforded.

Such tremendous love and gratitude come from the spirit babies to parents who experience stillbirth. **It's a strong mama who agrees to such a thing and in your baby's eyes, you're a HERO.**

Pregnancy After a Loss

Being pregnant after a loss comes with its own challenges, fear being the most prominent one. I remember so well when I got pregnant for the third time after my two miscarriages. I wouldn't let myself truly celebrate it or settle into it, for fear of having another miscarriage. Every time I went to the bathroom I was afraid I'd see blood. When we've suffered something traumatic, it's absolutely natural to be afraid of it happening again. The spirit babies want to help us move beyond that.

First off, the spirit babies encourage us to honor the sacred life experience we shared through the loss. Even though they are not attached to loss the same way we are with their higher perspective, they know that grief and mourning is a process we have to move through for full healing. So have a ceremony, light a candle, thank your baby for experiencing this with you and allow yourself to be open to the inherent gifts that your experience of loss brings. Perhaps do a meditation like I mentioned in the section "My First Prebirth Communication Experience" and exchange gifts with your baby. Honor your loss first before moving on. This closure can help dissipate any future fear.

Secondly, realize that no matter what we do, there will always be a little fear. It's natural and normal to feel a little fear, but we don't have to be ruled by it. The spirit babies tell us we should create a space for our fear, like a "fear jar" ~ a little container where we can place our fears, either physically or mentally. This is a powerful exercise because it allows us to acknowledge our fears instead of repressing them. Repressing fears just blows them up to bigger proportions. So, when we have a fear we can write it down and put it in the jar. It's saying to the fear, "I see you, I recognize you, I release you." We're bringing the fear out of us, up to the surface and containing it.

Then when we've contained our fear, we should come up with a counterpart ~ something true and beautiful that we can focus on. For example if the fear is, "I'm afraid I'm going to miscarry again," the counterpart would be, "I'm going to have an easy pregnancy and a beautiful baby." We should make that counterpart a regular part of our inner self talk. Repeating often until we truly believe it and feel it in every cell of our bodies.

The spirit babies tell us we should also affirm to ourselves that we don't need to learn through suffering anymore. We don't need to suffer, and we don't need to repeat past experiences or retrace our steps. It's true I had two miscarriages but it wasn't a repeat experience. They were very different and served very unique purposes that were meaningful to me. I also didn't have the benefit of the spirit baby wisdom back then that I do now. Back then I didn't know I could stop my suffering. I know that now. And so do you. **The time for suffering is over.**

Our spirit babies encourage us to create new patterns and new habits. Anything NEW we can do makes space for new energy to come in.

Most of all, talk to your baby. Tell your baby you understand that you're both now having a different experience. Tell your baby that you're allowing him or her to come in easily and healthy this time. Tell your baby that you are aligning with the highest possible outcome. Tell your baby you are done with suffering and you're ready to evolve through joyful experiences. Know you can have exactly what you want. Your baby is on board! That's what he or she wants too! You so got this.

Abortion
Abortion is such a heavy word. Women have been villainized for having them, adding to the guilt and sometimes regret associated with them. It's a controversial topic, one fraught with judgment and shame. When women have an abortion, it's a guilty secret they keep to themselves.

I'll never forget the first time I did a reading for someone who was considering an abortion. She'd sent me an email telling me that during a routine test, she was informed that her baby was testing positive for chromosomal abnormalities. She was devastated and considering abortion. She wanted me to connect with her baby to get his outlook on it.

WHAT ALL SPIRIT BABIES WANT THEIR MAMAS TO KNOW

Reading her email, the human part of myself was frantic (and honestly, perhaps a bit judgmental). My first thoughts were that this baby was coming bearing gifts. And even if it was challenging, they were challenges she had to face and if she didn't, she'd encounter the same challenges in different ways. The human part of me was trying to find a way to convince her that she had to keep this baby.

However, I knew I wasn't being fully objective, so I quieted my human mind and went to take a shower. It was in the shower that I started to hear the voice of her baby and what he said brought me to tears.

This wise and wonderful baby told me that there is absolutely no judgment about abortion in the spirit baby realm ~ that judgment against abortion is a human construct alone. He went on to tell me that often times abortion is a spiritual agreement between the spirit baby and the mother, to spark the mother into making a choice. A very significant and symbolic choice. The baby comes in briefly for the express purpose of having the mother make this difficult decision.

He said that the decision his mother was facing right now was really a huge opportunity to make an empowered choice ~ the choice of SELF-LOVE. This was paradigm shifting for me. Choosing abortion as an act of self-love?! Holy shit!

He went on to tell me that it's perfectly appropriate for a woman to decide she is not equipped to take on more than she's willing to FOR WHATEVER REASON. Placing those boundaries and drawing that particular line in the sand is a choice of empowerment, and often can be a turning point in the woman starting to put herself first.

After relaying these liberating messages from her spirit baby, this woman went forward with the abortion. Two months later she became pregnant again, this time with a healthy baby.

These expanded views of abortion have been repeated to me through many spirit babies, helping to ease the guilt, shame, and regret that many women who've aborted carry around with them.

Indeed, many of my most memorable and heart-expanding readings have been ones from spirit babies who've been "aborted" (I put that in quotes, because it doesn't even feel appropriate to use that term, knowing what I know). Another reading in particular really stands out for me.

A very distraught woman contacted me full of regret over a terminated pregnancy she'd had months before. She had two young children to care for as well as a very sick mother. Additionally she was looking for a job to help bring in money, since her husband had recently been fired. Despite all this, she initially was pleased with her newest pregnancy. Until a test showed that her daughter, if born, would have severe health issues and would need constant care. Abortion was not her first choice, as her family was religious and abortion was considered a sin. However after a couple of weeks of feeling like she was suffocating under a huge, heavy cloud, she and her husband decided she would have a secret abortion and tell everyone else it was a miscarriage. There was relief in this decision for both her and her husband...until the abortion was over.

Almost immediately afterwards she was overcome with guilt and regret, absolutely sure that she'd made the wrong decision, and should have sacrificed herself even more to give her very sick baby life. She was having nightmares and crying all the time, unable to forgive herself for "killing" her baby.

When tuning into her energy I immediately could see and feel a huge black heavy cloud acting like a barrier between her and her spirit baby. Her baby was still very much around her mama, trying to soothe her, comfort her and tell her she'd be back. But the woman was so overcome with guilt, shame, and regret that nothing was getting through. Thankfully this spirit baby was able to steer her mom to me so I could help lift that heavy cloud.

All her life this sensitive woman had been a care-taker, as evidenced in her home-life. She was taking care of her kids and her sick mother while also trying to find a job to help her husband. Not only was she a care-taker in this lifetime, she'd been a care-taker in many past lives. For centuries this woman had put everyone's needs in front of her own. She was very adept at sacrificing herself for others and that was a pattern she had to end. Now. Her spirit baby came in to help her do just that.

Her spirit baby showed me this was the most empowered decision her mama had ever made in ALL her lives and the very first time she had put her needs in front of anyone else's. And the fact she was able to put her needs first, even when it went against her religious beliefs, was symbolically significant ~ showing that she won't sacrifice herself anymore to anyone, not even to an unforgiving god. What this woman had actually done was clear lifetimes of karma and repression, by making this very difficult decision of saying "no, I absolutely will not take on any more hardships." It was more than huge. It was completely life altering.

This was the original agreement between the woman and her spirit baby, a "point of liberation" in her life chart, and she'd followed it to the letter. She'd done what she was supposed to do. She just had to UNDERSTAND it.

Her baby was celebrating the decision and off planning her next incarnation as a very healthy soul who would be a huge light in her mama's life. But the baby could not come through until her mother was able to move forward. This woman had fought the dragons she was supposed to fight, she just had to understand that the battle was over and she was indeed VICTORIOUS.

She had chosen SELF-LOVE with this abortion. And that changed everything.

As I was doing the reading I could see the huge, dark cloud of guilt, shame, and regret being lifted. It was so palpable, I was humbled. Her baby was right there, ready to come back. Her mama just had to lift up her head to see.

The messages from her spirit baby freed this mama's soul. She was able to see the expanded picture and understand that she'd played her role perfectly. All was exactly as it should be. And because she went through with this difficult decision of SELF-LOVE, her baby would come in again, but this time healthy and whole. Instead of having a karmic relationship based on hardship and care-taking, mama and baby will have a partnership based on joy and ease.

Three months later, her spirit baby came back.

So, is making the decision of "self-love" the case in all abortions? I truly don't know. It's the case with all the spirit babies I come in contact with. And if you've had an abortion and are reading these words, then it's true for you too.

It's more than a liberating concept. It's a revolutionary one.

Granted, as global consciousness expands, abortions will be a thing of the past, as will unplanned pregnancies. In the higher vibration babies will come in when invited, easily and without challenges. Until then and during our transitions, abortion can be an empowering tool for the soul's evolution ~ if we go in with our eyes, minds, and hearts wide-open, knowing we are being given an opportunity to put ourselves first. And no matter who else judges it, know that the spirit babies are celebrating their mothers every step of the way. Amen!

WHAT ALL SPIRIT BABIES WANT THEIR MAMAS TO KNOW

We Don't Have to "Earn" Our Babies

If we're having trouble conceiving or if we've experienced a loss, it's so easy to judge ourselves and think it's because of something we've done wrong. When I had my first miscarriage, one of my thoughts during my grieving process was that I hadn't really deserved my baby because it wasn't a planned pregnancy. It sounds silly saying it now, but it's a very real emotion that many mamas experience. Women who've had an abortion in the past can especially carry around this very heavy burden.

My game plan after my first miscarriage, when I started trying to conceive in earnest, was to do everything "right," so that this time I would be able to keep my baby. (Oh...I just want to give my past self a hug.) This time around I ate all the right things, I did cleanses every week, I did yoga regularly, I read all sorts of books on natural pregnancy and childbirth, and I even did my best to act the "right" way at all times, being extra helpful and considerate with everyone. When I finally became pregnant again five months later, I was ecstatic. This time I had "earned" my baby. I had done everything "right" and I knew he would stay.

Imagine how much worse the devastation was that time around when I miscarried my baby again. While my first miscarriage had broken my heart, this one shattered my world.

And it was important, significant, and exactly what needed to happen. I had too strong a hold on what was right or wrong, which is based on all sorts of false judgments. I thought I could "earn points" by doing things a certain way. I became a control freak of huge proportions, believing I could stop "bad things" happening by being a "good" person. **Basically, I thought if I could prove myself worthy I could get what I wanted.**

It's not my fault. It's no one's fault who feels like this. It's what we've been taught to believe all the way back to childhood and Santa Claus ~ if you act nice you get presents, if you act naughty you get shit. It's one of the lies of the old world that we must shed.

My second miscarriage didn't happen because I didn't deserve my baby. And it didn't happen just to prove me wrong or to punish me for believing in old worn-out lies. My miscarriage served me by shattering the world that was based on all those old beliefs. All at once the false truths were severed from my perception. In writing these words, I can now visualize the huge disconnect from lies and untruths that occurred then. And yes, it was painful. Man, it was painful! But it was a karmic severing from a past that was longer serving me and keeping me trapped. My second miscarriage, in essence, was an unshackling.

If I'd kept my baby instead of miscarrying, I would have carried those false beliefs forward into my parenting. It would have influenced my parenting and tampered with my child's freedom of expression. It would have been a lesser experience for my child and for me, and prevented us both from being higher versions of ourselves.

My miscarriage was a gift. It freed a large part of my energy as my truth was rearranged.

I didn't have to earn my baby by acting a certain way. I didn't have to deserve my baby by being a perfect person. I didn't have to be nice just so Santa would bring me a present.

It is our birthright to have our heart's desires. If it's part of our dream, it's part of our future. If we yearn for a baby it means there's a baby for us...and there's nothing we need to do to deserve it. **We are already worthy and more than enough just as we are.**

Healing a Traumatic Birth Experience

I've heard so many traumatic birth stories from new mamas. Too many. It used to make me enraged and I'd curse the medical industry for fucking it all up for everyone. Now while I still believe the medical industry fucks it all up for everyone, I now also know that it's appropriate and how it should be. I also know that it's changing.

With every other worn out system that doesn't serve our best interests, the medical industry is being forced to change. **Traumatic birth experiences are one of the catalysts for that change.**

As difficult as it is to hear, a traumatic birth is something we agreed to experience when planning our lives on the higher planes. Even our babies know what they're getting into when they sign up to be born a specific way. Our souls chose this experience for reasons we may not ever fully understand, but it's for reasons that make us stronger in many areas, and for the reasons of spiritual fast-tracking.

The predominant feeling that usually accompanies a traumatic birth is defeat. We feel like we did something wrong, that we weren't strong enough or capable enough. Traumatic birth can make us feel weak.

Dear Sister, nothing could be further from the truth. From the spirit baby perspective we are not weak AT ALL.

Only a very strong soul would agree to take on such an experience in order to be a catalyst for change. It is a bold and courageous soul decision to choose a traumatic birth. Only a true warrior can do it. Far from being weak, we are amazingly strong! In our babies' eyes, we are warrior goddesses! So we need to stop blaming ourselves for following our soul's plan to the letter.

Anger can also be a heavy feeling attached to traumatic birth. And surprisingly, the spirit babies say that not only is anger appropriate, but that it can act as fuel. It's perfectly appropriate to take on a stance of "I don't approve of what happened and I'm not going to stand for it anymore!" If we need to write a letter to the medical people who fucked it up by all means do so. Write a letter, confront someone, tell someone in charge. We have to do whatever we need to do to find closure. And then we need to move on.

Because after we move through the anger, we next need to embrace forgiveness. It may seem counter-intuitive to take an angered stance and then forgive, but they actually complement each other perfectly. And the spirit baby realm is HUGE on forgiveness.

In order to forgive, we truly have to understand that whatever we experienced was exactly what we were supposed to experience. All the people involved carried out the roles they were supposed to ~ even the people who fucked it up. **In the expanded perspective, everything is perfect.** Our bodies didn't let us down, the doctors didn't let us down, we didn't let ourselves down, and we didn't let our babies down. NOTHING WENT WRONG.

We can let go of judgment and blame as it was all scripted perfectly. We were following our highest path so we could become the highest versions of ourselves. And when we can actually mentally thank the people involved with the traumatic birth for carrying out their roles the way they did to help serve our higher purpose, that's when we know we've truly forgiven (and what a HUGE vibration raiser).

There is also no need to worry about our babies. Babies are not attached to the birth process as we are ~ especially not these very high vibrational babies. So we can let that go.

Now we know we chose to experience this because we are bad-ass warriors acting as change catalysts. We know that everything happened exactly as it should. And now we can forgive everyone involved because we know it served our highest purpose.

WHAT ALL SPIRIT BABIES WANT THEIR MAMAS TO KNOW

You won't have another traumatic birth. You don't have to repeat experiences or learn the same lesson twice. And especially now that you can see the higher perspective of your traumatic birth experience, you're free to make different choices and have better experiences.

You're a courageous bad-ass. Never forget it.

5

Spirit Baby Wisdom on Pregnancy and Birth

The Best Pregnancy Advice Ever

I hate traditional pregnancy advice. It absolutely drives me up a wall. Eat this many calories, exercise this much, avoid these foods, don't do these activities, gain this much weight. Arggggghhh! It's stupid! It's inane! And it's totally externally focused. This sort of advice takes the woman's natural intuition out of the equation and replaces it with numbers and arbitrary do's and don'ts. Most advice is based on fears and limitations. It's absolute bullshit.

And I'll tell you something else, the spirit babies laugh at the advice given to us by the so-called "experts." The spirit babies know it's ridiculous and totally focused in the wrong areas. So the first piece of advice we get from the spirit baby realm is throw out any advice that is rooted in limitation. Throw out any advice that diminishes our own intuition. Throw out any advice that tells us to be afraid.

WHAT ALL SPIRIT BABIES WANT THEIR MAMAS TO KNOW

The best advice we can get is from our own bodies, our own babies, and our own intuition. It's an inside job and it has nothing to do with calories consumed (grrrrrr.....). Our bodies will tell us what we need to eat, when, and how much. And it might be different every day. Some days we might want to eat six meals all with bacon as the main ingredient. Some days we might want to eat two meals of salads. It doesn't matter. We need to forget everything we've been taught about traditional nutrition (because let's face it, it changes all the time and no one has gotten any healthier) and simply listen to our bodies. Period.

The spirit babies also tell us not to rely too heavily on testing. Routine prenatal testing often causes more problems than solving them. Tests have their place, but we should use them only to validate our own intuition, not to inform us. If we want to know if our baby is okay, we should ask him or her. We can say "Hey Baby, if you're doing okay, give me a kick," or "Hey Baby, if there's something I need to know, send me a dream." We need to turn inward, be still and silent, and allow our intuition to be our true guide. If we do choose to have tests, we can inform our babies what is happening and why and even ask for the outcome we'd prefer.

The spirit baby realm also encourages us to surround ourselves with supportive people, including our doctors or midwives. Don't be afraid to switch or make waves if someone is not resonating with you. We are the ones in charge of our pregnancies and anyone who treats us otherwise should be fired or at least put in their place.

After a couple of horrible appointments with doctors during my first two pregnancies (which ended in miscarriage) I found a lovely midwife whom I really liked. I was with her for the first 20 weeks of my pregnancy. But then, even though I really liked her and respected her, I noticed every time I left an appointment I was feeling like my intuition had diminished. It wasn't intentional on her part, but it still didn't sit right with me. Especially because at the time, I was leaning toward unassisted homebirth, and we weren't seeing eye-to-eye.

It was with great difficulty that I ended up writing her a letter telling her I was done with her services while thanking her for all she'd done. It was an important, empowering moment for me. This was not someone who'd pissed me off or wronged me in any way. In fact I adored her. But she was making me question myself and I was unwilling to experience that any longer. It was the right decision for me and I was left to explore my inner wisdom unfettered the rest of my pregnancy. (Thankfully, my midwife eventually understood my decision and came to visit after my baby was born.)

I'm not encouraging anyone to forgo professional services or prenatal care, I'm just saying we should look at those things as supplemental. We can allow our pregnancies to be easy, uneventful, and joyful. And the less interference the better.

And finally, the spirit baby realm encourages us to talk to them as much as we can during pregnancy. Look for signs, dreams, totems, and messages ~ we are getting them constantly. We can communicate with them in a special journal or we can meditate with them. There is a universe of infinite wisdom available to us from our spirit babies. Remember, they can act as guides from their birds-eye-view and help steer us in the direction of our highest potentials.

By turning within and listening to our bodies, our babies, and our intuition we'll get all the advice we need. We'll know what to eat, how to move, which people to surround ourselves with, what kind of birth we'll benefit from, and so much more.

The absolute best advice when it comes to pregnancy: LISTEN TO OUR BABIES. We'll be surprised, delighted, and perhaps even enlightened by what we hear.

Getting Ready for Your Empowered Birth

I have a confession to make. I used to be a birth-judger. I used to believe that only natural births were the "good" births and I sheepishly admit that I'd get slightly angry at women who succumbed to c-section births, thinking they were copping out.

Now it's not entirely my fault. When I was researching unassisted homebirth for my first birth, all the books were very judgy about hospitals and doctors, pointing out all the ways these so-called "experts" really made things worse by creating problems, hijacking what could have been beautiful births.

With the huge rising numbers of c-section births in recent decades, there's now been a large swing in the other direction toward the natural birth movement. With that movement toward natural methods, there's inevitably judgment about the not-so-natural methods. I find that people are most judgmental when they are changing belief structures. In many ways judgment is a defense mechanism, and maybe even an appropriate one. In order to change our perception to something new, to what we now believe is "right," it's easier for us to judge the thing we're moving away from as "wrong."

With my own first birth experience I was making the mental swing from "Give me the epidural, I'm nobody's hero!" to doing it all on my own, with no doctor or midwife present. Quite a huge swing. I had to be judgmental to help build my confidence.

So perhaps we can look at judgment not as a bad thing, but simply as a tool that people use when they're building confidence and finding new footing. Once we have confidence and are firmly rooted, we no longer need the judgment, and we can be free to let others live the way they want without letting it impact us. (If only everyone got that memo about judgment, huh?)

In any case, I'm now a reformed birth judger. I've realized you can have an empowered birth no matter how or where it's done. What changed me was when I was collecting birth stories for my website years ago. One woman sent me the most beautiful birth story. It had me in tears. And it was a c-section birth. Totally blew my mind.

And of course, working so closely with the spirit baby realm and having access to their expanded wisdom makes it impossible to judge anything as wrong or bad. **According to the spirit babies, any choice can be empowered if we enter into it consciously.**

So many women come to me asking "How does my baby want to be born?" The answer from the spirit baby is always "However my mama feels most comfortable." This is a liberating answer, as it takes the pressure off having to give birth a certain way. Because, let's face it, with the swing to the natural birth movement, there is a lot of pressure. And if we're unable to give birth naturally, there's also a lot of disappointment. And the LAST thing we need is to enter into motherhood thinking we've already failed.

Now, in the higher vibration, birth will be very different. It won't be medicalized at all and will be much easier for every woman and baby. But during our transition, we can still use these methods and make empowered decisions.

Many people think that because I had three unassisted homebirths that's how I'd recommend everyone do it. Far from it. If a woman thinks unassisted homebirth is crazy and irresponsible, then she certainly shouldn't attempt it. Others think me incredibly brave. Honestly though, back then I was very energetically impressionable. I would take on other people's energies and internalize it. I knew I would not be able to fully concentrate on my own birth process without taking on the energy of everyone else in the room. I even kicked my husband out.

WHAT ALL SPIRIT BABIES WANT THEIR MAMAS TO KNOW

For the longest time I thought my first spirit baby had directed me toward unassisted homebirth because that's how HE needed to be born. It wasn't until years later, when communing with the spirit baby realm, that I realized he had directed me toward unassisted homebirth because **that's how I needed to give birth.** That's how I felt the safest. And he knew it better than I.

Your spirit baby can do that for you too. So instead of asking your baby "how do you want to be born?", look inside yourself to see how you'd feel the most comfortable and the safest giving birth. Then your baby will help guide you to that empowered choice.

One thing the spirit babies want us to take into consideration when deciding how to give birth is the support around us. Birth is a very personal and sacred thing, it should be treated as such for the mother's benefit as much as for the baby's. If we want an empowered birth, we need to surround ourselves with empowering people. And while I still feel that's challenging to find in hospitals (okay, perhaps I haven't let go of all judgments), it is possible to find a doctor who'll support us. If you feel safest giving birth in a hospital, shop around until you find the right doctor. Don't settle for the first one you're given, just because that was the one available. Find one that's a good fit.

No matter where you're giving birth, whether it's a hospital, birth center or at home, shop around until you find the right support person. Not every midwife involved in the natural birth movement is necessarily empowering either. If someone is making you feel sick instead of pregnant, that's not your support person. If someone is placing fear or limits on you, that's not your support person. If someone is focusing more on what could go wrong, that's not your support person. The right person will support your desires as well as enhance them and cheerlead them.

So shop around. You are in charge. That's the attitude your baby encourages you to have. This is the work of your intuition, your desires, your body, and your baby. You're the one running the show. Everyone else is the support cast. You are woman, let's hear you roar!

Okay, now that we know we're in charge and NO ONE ELSE, let's look at other particulars. It's good to have intentions about the birth, but we shouldn't put too much focus on the outcomes. For instance, it's best to say to yourself "My birth will be an empowering peak experience," rather than "I'll have a 5 hour labor and a natural birth." You may very well have a 5 hour labor and a natural birth, but it's the FEELINGS around the birth that you should focus on. Because, as we've already discovered, you can have a c-section birth and still have an empowering peak experience.

Of course, you should decide where and how you want to give birth based on your preferences. If you want a natural birth at home, then intend it and plan for it, but don't attach yourself to it. Open up to it and trust it will all unfold as it should. When planning for my unassisted homebirth, I did whatever I could to prepare for it. I also had emergency numbers by the phone just in case. It helped alleviate the pressure. And ironically when we take the pressure off the outcome we truly want, that's the outcome we usually get.

During my third pregnancy, I developed a migraine at week 38. And this was a 24/7 round-the-clock migraine. I could find no relief ~ it was utter agony. I tried acupuncture, a chiropractor, a doctor, cranial-sacral therapy, and energy work to help alleviate it. All to no avail. I was in constant pain and I was getting exhausted.

I was in-tune enough to understand that some karmic stuff was getting worked through during this two week long headache and I let my baby and my inner voice guide me through the clearing. One of the things I knew I had to explore was the idea of giving birth a different way. I'd had two unassisted births previously and had planned another one with this baby, but I had to come to terms with the fact that I might need help. The pain from my endless migraine was taking up all of my energy and making my body weak. I truly didn't know if I'd have the strength to give birth on my own.

I understood that my karmic clearing may have to do with having a c-section, and while it scared the shit out of me, I knew I had to explore the possibility. Perhaps it was my turn to have an empowered c-section in a hospital. So, in a fit of bravery, I went to visit a doctor to share my situation and ask for help. At first she was hesitant to take me on so late in my pregnancy, especially since I'd had no prenatal care. But she finally relented and said she'd be there if I needed her. I was surprised to leave feeling exalted! I knew what I wanted, a third unassisted homebirth, but I had opened myself to other ways, knowing I could feel empowered no matter what. And that felt good.

Around week 40 my headache started to dissipate. It was a Sunday and the doctor I'd visited called me to say "Kate, if you can stay home to give birth, do it. You'd only have a power-struggle here." I appreciated her honesty and took it as a sign that I'd give birth the way I preferred. Opening up to a different possibility helped bring out the outcome I truly wanted.

I went into labor that night and had my third peak birth experience, unassisted and at home.

So INTEND but don't attach. Attaching creates control issues, and we know those never work out in our favor. Focus on how you want to FEEL about your birth experience and then let it unfold organically on it's own. It's truly about intending it, and then getting the hell out of the way.

Birth plans can be a good way to make intentions, but again focus on the FEELINGS rather than the particulars. "I'll have a beautiful, empowered birth which will be peak experience and I'll give birth to a healthy, amazing baby." That's a good place to start. And end.

You can also communicate with your baby throughout the birth. The reason that first empowered c-section story I mentioned moved me to tears was because this mama stayed in constant communication with her baby throughout, either out-loud or telepathically. She was a gentle source of love and wisdom, telling her baby what was happening the whole time, already proving herself an infinitely wise, attuned mama.

I did a reading recently where a woman was feeling defeated because she was sure she'd have to have another c-section birth since she'd had one the first time around. After giving her the whole "you're in charge" and "find people to support you, not bring you down" speech from her spirit baby, I told her that even if she did have to have another c-section, she could stay in constant communication with her baby. She could still connect with him even if he was in another room. It was important to the baby that his mama give birth in the way SHE felt safest, and also important the she knew she could talk to him the whole time. This alleviated so much pressure for her. It lifted the feelings of defeat and despair. In the end she found different support people, and rather than having a traumatic c-section, like the one she had previously, she had a very healing and beautiful natural birth in a birth center.

So, Dear Sister, to sum up:

- Find people who support your empowerment.
- Plan, intend, but don't attach.
- Focus on feelings, rather than details.
- Know you can communicate with your baby the whole time.

And now, get ready for your empowered birth!

6

When We Get Prebirth Communication "Wrong"

It is possible to have prebirth communication with one spirit baby and then end up giving birth to another. It's rare that this happens, but it's definitely not out of the realm of possibilities. However, even when this happens it doesn't mean we truly got anything "wrong." We weren't talking to the wrong spirit baby, and we didn't give birth to the wrong baby. **We were getting the exact information we were meant to have in order to fulfill our part of the soul contract with our baby (or babies).**

I recently heard from a woman who was sure she was pregnant with her daughter, but when she gave birth it was to a boy. In hindsight, she realized she was also having communication with the boy through dreams, but it wasn't as vivid as with her daughter, so she'd discounted it. As I tuned in, I was able to ascertain that the daughter had delayed her incarnation due to a situation that had changed in her mother's life which now gave the daughter higher opportunities for soul-evolution if she waited a bit longer. So she and a spirit baby intended for later (her future brother) agreed to switch birth order.

A lot of things can occur during pregnancy that we have no reference for. Spirit babies can have "energetic twins" where one spirit baby acts as a support system for the other during pregnancy but doesn't plan on being born. This can confuse prebirth communication, because an attuned mama can feel both spirit babies. Gender switching can also happen in pregnancy, where either a baby decides to change the gender he or she originally was going to incarnate as, or the actual spirit baby switches with another spirit baby. It's easy to discount these occurrences or deny they can happen since there's no tangible proof. But when ultrasounds get it wrong, often it's due to gender switching. Remember nothing is impossible in the spirit baby realm.

I have intimate experience with both energetic twins and gender switching in the womb. My third pregnancy I was pregnant with my daughter but gave birth to a son.

I didn't know if I was going to include this story as it's so personal and so dear to my heart. I've only told a handful of people the full story of my third pregnancy and birth, because it seems so impossible. It's easy for any skeptic to say I just got the prebirth communication "wrong." However, I'm so rooted in my own truth and knowing, that it doesn't matter if anyone believes my story or not. It's true for me. And it's true for my husband, who had quite a bit of prebirth communication with this baby, which helped us put the pieces of the puzzle together when we thought we got it "wrong." It's a beautiful story and one I'm now ready to tell everyone.

When Getting It "Wrong" is the Highest Path
My first two sons had both come out exactly the way they'd told me they would. They looked like they did in my dreams, and they had the

personality traits I dreamt they would. So when I had my first communication with a girl spirit baby, I didn't doubt for a moment that it was my daughter.

I had never actively wanted a daughter. I was very happy and complete with my two sons. I thought I was done having children. It was when my second boy was four months old and I was packing up some newborn clothes we weren't using anymore that my daughter came to me and whispered "Keep those pajamas for me when I come." I dreamt of her that night. She was dark-haired, dimpled, and she told me her name was Lilah.

She was such a beautiful soul, and there was already such a connection between the two of us, that I agreed to have her come in, but told her she'd need to wait a bit. I continued to have many dreams about her the next two years and it was the strongest communication I'd ever had. She told me her favorite colors, that she wanted to play the piano, that she liked horses. Our whole family knew about her. So when I got pregnant, it was like welcoming Lilah home.

Nine weeks into my pregnancy my husband and I shared a dream. On the same night we both dreamt of twins, a boy and a girl. In my dream I was told that the baby boy wouldn't be sticking around but was here as support. That was the first time I got information about "energetic twins." In my husband's dream the boy came along with the girl. And frankly, it scared the crap out him. Being seasoned parents we knew how much work babies can be, and we didn't desire twins. Due to my dream, however, I didn't worry too much about it.

Over the course of my pregnancy the communication with my daughter continued strong. And not just for me. Seven of my friends (seven!) dreamt of my baby girl and she looked the same to all of them. Two intuitives also tuned into my baby and validated that it was my daughter. I was 100% sure that my baby was a girl. There was no room for doubt.

While I was pregnant I was also strangely compelled to adopt a dog. I'd been looking for a dog almost as long as I was waiting for my daughter to come. It feels strange to talk about a dog and a spirit baby together in the same story, and I honestly still don't understand the full connection, but it's significant so bear with me. My husband told me I was crazy to want a new dog while also expecting a baby but I could not be deterred. Along with spirit babies, I'd been dreaming about dogs and knew one was meant to be ours. We knew we didn't want a puppy because we'd have a newborn, so we were looking at rescue dogs. Twice we'd thought we'd found our dog, but it was never the right fit. We had to wait awhile longer.

The pregnancy with my daughter was such an easy one. I was the most active I'd ever been while being pregnant, running every other day. I had energy, vitality, and felt incredibly healthy. Until week 38.

On a Tuesday evening I came home from a day at the beach with my boys and while starting to prepare dinner I got a very sharp pain in the back of my neck. I grabbed the edge of the sink to support myself as the pain shot from my neck to my head. And stayed there. It was so severe and so persistent that after an hour and a half, I had my husband drive me to the emergency clinic. I wasn't worried for myself as much as I was for my baby.

The baby was monitored and I was given aspirin but unless I wanted a cat-scan there was nothing they could do for me. My baby was all right, that's all I needed to know. I decided to go home and deal with the pain, sure it would be gone the next day.

But it wasn't gone the next day, nor the next. Four days into this endless migraine I realized that there was more going on here than just a headache. I understood that a huge chunk of karma was being worked out and I was cleansing stuff from my energetic field. I tuned into to myself, looked at old patterns and ideas that needed to change, and did everything I could to expand myself.

Working through my fears of having anything but an unassisted home-birth was definitely part of it (as mentioned in detail in the section "Getting Ready for Your Empowered Birth"). Finding the ability within myself to ask for help was also a major part of the equation. I'd always had one of those independent-I can-do-it-myself attitudes, but now I needed help ~ help from others to ease my pain and help from friends to take care of my boys. Allowing myself to be helped was a big piece of my karmic clearing. But the largest part, even though I didn't know it at the time, was in letting go of my daughter ~ the daughter I'd been talking to for three years.

A midwife I'd gone to when I was seeking alternatives to an unassisted homebirth, suggested that I might want to open up to the fact that my daughter could actually be a boy. She thought my headache might be related to my certainty that my baby was a girl. I wasn't convinced, but in an effort to get rid of my headache I decided to entertain the idea.

A few nights later, I had my husband and two young boys all sit in a circle with me. We lit a candle and talked to Lilah. I told her I loved her and had enjoyed our connection the past three years, but if she needed to be born a boy that was okay with us. More than anything we just wanted her to be healthy. We all took turns inviting her to be a boy. Looking back, I know that was a very important ceremony.

Despite all my attempts at alleviating my head pain, nothing worked. Until week 40, when a couple of days after our ceremony, my headache started to dissipate on its own. It was a Saturday night and I was lying in bed with my hands on my belly, when all of a sudden, there was a flurry of activity in my womb, and the most blissful feelings came over me. A blanket of peace settled around me as I was filled with the feeling of absolute grace. I knew that, no matter what, everything was going to be okay. I'm now convinced that was when my babies switched.

That night I dreamt I gave birth to a boy.

The next day I went into labor and had a peaceful unassisted homebirth to a dark-haired, dimpled baby who turned out to be a son.

Despite the ceremony and the dream of birthing a boy, I was still bewildered and confused. Why had I been talking to Lilah for three years and now delivered a boy? A stranger whose name I didn't even know?

Thankfully newborns are easy to love. My newest son had such a peaceful presence and joyful energy that I was immediately enamored. I also knew that he was a brave warrior to come in completely unannounced when he knew I was expecting someone else. It was effortless falling in love with him. But even as I did, I knew I had to mourn my daughter. I'd had a relationship with this soul for three years and now I wouldn't even meet her. At one point I was really angry with her and I went outside, away from everyone else, and raged at her. I could still hear her around me and she said "Give me your anger. It is appropriate and I can take it. Soon you'll understand." I was mollified.

When my baby boy was about a week old, my husband and I were having a conversation where I was wondering out loud why Lilah had decided not to come. It was then my husband told me about some dreams he'd had when I was pregnant. Dreams he'd kept from me because they scared him.

He said "I have to tell you, when I saw we had another boy I was relieved." Then he relayed to me the recurring dream he had while I was pregnant, where there was something really wrong with our daughter. He was sure that had she come in, she would have been very sick.

WHAT ALL SPIRIT BABIES WANT THEIR MAMAS TO KNOW

That jogged my memory of a dream I'd had of a very sick daughter when I was pregnant with my second son. It had unsettled me for weeks. I started to wonder if we were starting to get pieces of the puzzle.

A couple of weeks later my family and I were in a new age store where they were offering psychic readings. I brought my baby in with me and asked about him. It was then validated to me that there was still a girl hanging around us, but had she come in at that point she would have been born very sick with a "missing strand." I was told that our baby boy had come instead because it would make life "so much easier and joyful."

Another reading from a different intuitive also picked up on this theme. I was told again that my daughter wasn't supposed to have come in this time around because she would have been very sick. In fact she'd been my sick daughter in many of my lifetimes and it was time for that karmic loop to end.

With all these pieces of the puzzle I've been able to put the story together in a way that truly resonates with me. My daughter started coming to me as part of our soul contract so we could clear lifetimes of illness. The reason our connection was so strong right away is because we've been connected before in many past lives.

When I got pregnant with her, she brought in her energetic twin, knowing that he was not only support for her but that if things followed the highest path of potential, he'd be taking her place. Both my husband and I had dreamt of her twin. In my dream he went away, but in reality she did.

That two week headache I had was where we all made huge energetic leaps and bounds. So much karma was cleared during that time period (where I took on the sickness and allowed myself to be helped) that my daughter was able to stop her karmic loop of coming in ill. Instead of getting a very sick daughter, I got a very healthy, joyful boy.

I admit that to others this explanation could appear to be a case of sour grapes. And if all that karma was cleared then why couldn't Lilah just come in healthy instead of sending another baby in her place? I can't pretend that I have all the knowledge of the inner workings of the spirit baby realm. All I know is that it happened exactly the way it should have and we followed the highest path. To me it's a beautiful story.

My daughter is still in the spirit world. We thought we may ask her in at some point but we actually feel complete as a family. She won't go to anyone else, she's happy playing on the Other Side. She knew her highest role was to work through the karma with me and that was fulfilled. She's free to do whatever she wants now. I don't feel like she's missing and I don't have a yearning for her. Our story is complete. And exactly as it should be.

My third son is an absolute bright, shining light. He's one of the new children who came in with no karma and no baggage. He's a true master and I look to him often for inspiration. Yet it's funny, whenever I talk about him being in my belly or talk of being pregnant with him, it doesn't feel right. Although he was in my energetic field when I was pregnant, I just KNOW he was never in my belly until the switch happened the day before I gave birth. I was never truly pregnant with him. Which makes him even more of a miracle.

Oh, and when my baby boy was five months old, we found our rescue dog. She came to us with the name, "Lilah."

Part Two

7

Your Vibrational Journey

All my spirit baby readings group themselves into two parts. For the first half of the reading the baby is offering wisdom on why things have happened the way they have. Comfort, relief, and an expanded perspective is given to the mama as she begins to understand that everything has been perfectly orchestrated, and she's played her role perfectly. The second half of the reading is where the spirit baby takes on the role of life coach and aids the mama in refining her vibration. Her soul, of course, is in charge of the whole journey and she'd get there on her own, but having the added benefit of the voice of her spirit baby, who acts as both guide and cheerleader, is an amazing amplifier. When the voice of our spirit babies join forces with the voice of our souls, our paths illuminate in the most magical ways.

The rest of this book is about your vibrational journey, and what you can do, from your spirit baby's point of view, to make great leaps in frequency.

Awakening to LOVE

There are many things going on simultaneously while our consciousness is expanding. Our frequency is changing to a higher vibration, our mind is being rewired, and we are being disconnected from the old matrix based on limitations and fear. Even our physical bodies have no choice but to change into a higher version of themselves (often called "lightbodies").

There are many sources available now that talk of ascension, enlightenment, and lightbody activation so I'm not going to explain it all here, but I will briefly describe some things that may occur while we are awakening. First off, awakening simply means that we are waking from our human amnesia and remembering the truth of who we really are ~ we are limitless, joyful, and wildly creative beings. Up until now we've been creating under the oppression of fear and the need for sources outside of ourselves to provide for us. That is all radically changing. As we awaken, we remember that LOVE is the true source. We discover that it comes from within, and that it is self-sustainable. When we start to create from our inner self-sustainable LOVE, everything around us starts to look and feel quite different.

What Limitlessness Looks Like

Years ago I had what can only be called an "initiation" into this limitless state of being and it changed me forever. The date was 11/11/11, a very significant, symbolic date. Somehow I knew SOMETHING AMAZING was going to happen that day, even if I didn't know what it was. I spent all day in anticipation of greatness. And while it did turn out to be a very nice day, nothing truly out of the ordinary happened. That is, until later that night, when my husband and I made love. Immediately afterwards, as I was lying in his arms, SOMETHING AMAZING happened.

I was given a very clear vision of how I'd been holding everything at arm's length my whole life. I'd been having surface experiences and surface relationships. Even the people closest to me, I did not fully let in. It was appropriate for my human experience up until that time. I did it by means of protection. My whole life purpose had been about keeping myself safe and protected.

Then I was shown how life would be if I truly immersed myself into it ~ how intimate, beautiful, and truly joyful it would be. It was only later I fully understood what had taken place ~ at that moment when SOMETHING AMAZING happened, my soul had descended into my body. What I was being shown was the division of life before and after my soul and I were united as one.

This is truly the aim of our awakening ~ to raise our vibrations to such a degree that our souls can fully join with us and we can live out our lives as divine humans.

I spent three blissful weeks fully joined with my soul. It was an entirely different existence. I was fearless for one. And man, just that alone would have been enough! I vividly remember the first time I went to the grocery with my soul fully intact. I was bringing home things for my boys I wouldn't have brought home before ~ things with artificial colors and flavors. I remember thinking "What was I so afraid of before?" The fear felt ridiculous! Fear in any form is impossible when you're united with your soul. Your soul knows you need no protection from anything and that nothing "bad" can happen.

I also wasn't afraid of lack. Lack wasn't even a concern. I went into my local co-op and the owner told me they were struggling to keep afloat. Without even thinking, I handed her $150. It's not like I had a whole bunch of money in my account, but it didn't even matter. My soul knew that money was simply energy, and it would come back around when I needed it. Can you imagine the FREEDOM in not worrying about money?

Being joined with my soul was also so impacting on my mothering. Instead of being overwhelmed with 3 young boys, I was ready to take on ANYTHING. I remember declaring one night "I could have 10 kids and absolutely LOVE it!" I was so interested in what my boys were doing. I would sit next to my oldest boy on the couch, watching him play his Nintendo 3DS and be totally rapt, instead of just feigning interest. I would read to them for hours and be completely immersed in the books with them, rather than just flicking through the pages as fast as I could. I would throw them on the bed over and over for hours simply for the JOY of it. There were whole new exciting universes to explore just in my very own home!

The creativity was flowing out of me in new, exciting ways and I was compelled to follow through. At one point I just HAD to run outside for a piece of tree bark so I could paint the word "Bliss" on it. And yes...I was blissful.

Everything felt like a celebration. "Yay! I get to fill the sugar bowl! Yay! I get to empty the dishwasher!" Even the mundane had become interesting! Can you imagine THAT? I wanted to celebrate everything because everything was wonderful. In the evenings my husband would ask me if I wanted a beer and I'd say "I don't need one, I'm high on life! But YES I'll have one, because let's celebrate!"

One of the best perks of being united with my soul was feeling absolutely at home no matter where I was. I was as comfortable out in the world as I was sitting at home on my living room couch. I was doing things and going places I wouldn't have done or gone to before, because I could handle ANYTHING. Home came with me, home WAS me, no matter where I went.

My interactions with others were spontaneous and playful and damn, I was freakin' funny! There was also an effortless ability to observe others and not be drawn in by their drama. In fact, I could actually SEE why the drama was happening for the person, how it was serving them, and the perfection of it all. I could also see the larger roles they were playing and how truly AMAZING they were.

Another surprising side effect of being joined with my soul was that I didn't need to eat! The LOVE lighting my being from my soul had made me truly self-sustainable and I didn't need to rely on outside sources to nourish me. I often forgot to eat because I just didn't need to, but when I did eat it was solely for the purpose of pleasure. With this also came the knowledge that my body knew exactly what to do with any food it was given and that it could automatically self-correct and self-harmonize. There was no need to worry about nutrition ~ my body could handle a hot fudge sundae as easily as it could handle an apple. I was told that very soon people would come to understand that food doesn't have to be related to weight or health. When we're in a higher vibration, food is SIMPLY for pleasure! Imagine the FREEDOM that comes with THAT, Sister!

And speaking of weight. At that time I had a 3-month-old baby and about 15 pounds of postpartum weight. With my soul lighting up all my cells, the weight was falling effortlessly off me.

Everything was exciting, everything was worth celebrating. I couldn't wait to wake up each morning and engage with my day. I felt better than a kid on Christmas morning. I had no fears, no worries, no drama, and there was nothing I couldn't do. Life was joyful, amazing, blissful, and exciting!

Being united with my soul changed every single aspect of my life. I knew that once everyone could feel this way, then the world we live in would change very, VERY quickly.

I had the blessing of being united with my soul the whole rest of November. And then, all at once on December 1st, the door was shut. My soul retreated and I was left in utter darkness.

I'll never forget the initial blackness I felt the day my soul receded. I couldn't even look at my precious children. Instead I had to escape to my room. While tuning in to myself to make sense of what happened I was told "You've now been shown what life is like when you're reunited with your soul. This was a gift given to you. Now... get there yourself."

I have to admit it was a frustrating answer. I'd already been utterly devoted to my spiritual journey for years! I'd already been through trials and tribulations and expanded myself in so many ways! I thought I had "made it"! Now I was being told there was still more more work to do.

But now I also knew it would be worth it. Feeling like that on a permanent basis would be worth ANYTHING. So I devoted myself again to my vibrational journey with a renewed fervor. Each day I do what I can to embody love to my fullest extent, even as I'm homesick for my soul.

Five years later, large pieces of my limitlessness have made their way through. So much has changed and, more often than not, I feel many of the same sensations as I did when I was fully reunited. But I am not yet fully reunited. Thankfully I'm at a place in my vibrational journey where I'm much more comfortable with the pace of it all. I'm in a space of absolute trust in myself. Which, after a three year period of "the dark night of the soul," is quite a relief!

The reunion with my soul is imminent. Of that I'm sure. And each day I continue to devote myself to my vibration until my soul brings HOME back to me for good.

Frequency Jumping
First off, I want to point out again that the vibrational journey to our souls is a NATURAL one that takes place organically. You're already on it and you've simply chosen this book as part of your journey to remembering. I'm really not telling you anything new, I'm simply helping to

spark what you already know. Your soul is fully in charge of your evolution and knows exactly what it's doing.

All that being said, embodying love and raising our vibrations may not look like we think it should. It has nothing to do with being a perfect person, who never experiences negative emotions. During my "limitlessness initiation," I still sometimes got mad and yelled at my kids, but then I laughed about it immediately after, and there was no guilt attached. In a higher vibration we will sometimes still feel negative emotions (and we'll definitely feel them along the way!), but we won't be attached to them.

I'm going to cover some of the basic information that the spirit babies often share with their mamas in readings regarding the vibrational journey. (If you want to know more about the topics in the following chapters, I cover each one extensively in my "Awakening Series" videos found on lovefrombaby.com)

Basically it all comes down to one simple word: NEW. In order to embody a new energy we have to do things in different ways. Here are some areas that we need to bring the NEW into:

- Our Self-Talk: It's important that we pay attention to the stories we're telling ourselves in our heads. Are we being our best friends and our own head cheerleaders? Or are we telling ourselves constantly what's wrong. Changing our self-talk to something positive helps to rewire our brains in new and better ways. Our minds are very busy and constantly chattering away at us, usually with not very useful stuff. One of my favorite things to do, for the sake of retraining my brain, is to come up with a simple affirmation and use it whenever my loquacious mind won't shut the hell up. My affirmations usually last a week or so, until they lose their luster, then I'll come up with a new one. Often times (because I've been doing this forever) I'll bring old ones back and recirculate them. Affirmations should be short, simple, and full of loving TRUTH. The truth is simple. It's only the false beliefs, fears, and limits that are lengthy. I'll share some of my favorites:

"I love myself, I love myself, I love myself." This one is a go-to for any situation. If I need comfort, building up, distractions or a hug I'll just "love myself" repeatedly.

"Everything happens for the best and everything happens for a reason." I came in knowing this one and used it as a kid when things didn't go the way I wanted. I knew I didn't have to understand why something happened, I just had to accept it was serving higher purposes and everything would eventually work out. And probably better than I expected. I still use it often.

"I am magnificently beautiful!" I use this one when I'm feeling old, ugly, or squishy. I'll also use it when I'm feeling beautiful, because we should encourage our beauty!

"Everyone's path is perfect." I use this when I'm feeling judgy about someone else's choices or decisions. We have to understand that everyone is doing the best they can.

I could go on and on. I have one for every situation. Come up with your own, personalize them, and use them often. A quiet mind is a beautiful thing, but since that's not our reality we can at least redirect with simple, loving truths over and over and over and over...

- Embracing ALL our Emotions: While it would be lovely to only be happy all the time (and frankly, we've been taught that if we're not happy, there's something wrong with us) that's just not the reality of things. We're humans and we came here to experience the whole spectrum of human emotions. We may as well embrace them. Embracing all of our emotions, without judgment is a HUGE vibrational jumper.

The trap with emotions like anger or sadness is the secondary emotion we create around the anger or sadness. Anger or sadness, in and of themselves, serve a specific purpose. But when we're feeling guilty or ashamed about feeling anger or sadness, that's where we get lost. I can't tell you how many times I've gotten angry at myself for being angry! And it's ridiculous. Anger is an emotion we can use as fuel if we tap in and listen to it. But getting angry at our anger, creates a secondary emotion that keeps us down and out. Secondary emotions make the primary emotions stick to us, often for a long time. Whereas if we allow ourselves to feel the primary emotion WITHOUT GUILT OR JUDGMENT, it will pass through us rather quickly.

It's not the anger or sadness we need to get rid of, it's the secondary self-degrading emotion we create around it. Now instead of getting angry that I'm angry, I stop for a minute to see what the anger is telling me. There's information there and often times whatever I'm angry at is something I have the power to change right away. Anger is a GREAT fuel and can be very productive.

Now, something that I have to mention is that often times on a spiritual journey we're clearing, cleansing and purifying so much that long lost emotions will come to the surface for reasons we don't understand. It's not important to always understand why we are having an emotion, but it's always important to embrace it. When we are able to hold more LIGHT, the little dark shadows will be illuminated. Hold those dark little shadows close to you like a little teddy bear that's simply craving love. So many times I've said to the feelings coming to the surface "Oh hello Sadness, come on in. You're beautiful and I love you." I don't need to know where the sadness is coming from (sometimes it's simply impossible to know), I just have to understand that it's coming up to be loved.

The spirit babies would LOVE their mamas to have the ability of unconditionally loving any emotion. When we can do that for ourselves, it's so much easier to do for everyone else, especially our children. Adults who can't handle their own intense emotions have no chance of handling their children's intense emotions.

Embracing all of our emotions is not only a way of making huge vibrational leaps, it's a tremendous gift for our children as well.

- Upgrading our Relationships: This one almost ALWAYS comes up in spirit baby readings, even amongst parents who already have a great relationship. I was doing a reading recently where this topic came up and the cheeky spirit baby interrupted the reading to tell ME I should also take this advice. I'd been outed.

Absolutely everyone can use this advice. No matter how good a relationship is, upgrades always help. The relationship between their mama and papa is very important to the spirit babies. It's the primary relationship the baby will witness and learn from. So many times when a baby is born, the relationship between parents takes a backseat. Even when we try so hard to make sure that doesn't happen, often times it's inevitable. We should always be looking for ways to upgrade because the spirit babies tell me they certainly don't want to be the cause for distance between the two people they love most. A relationship upgrade is a great frequency jumper, and not only does it benefit the people in the relationship, everyone around them benefits as well.

To upgrade a relationship bring the NEW into it. Look for new things to do together, talk to each other in more loving ways, create new habits, new patterns. New, new, new. You don't have to do everything new. Even just choosing one new thing to do together is enough to make space for new energy to come in.

Even if you can't get your partner on board for upgrades, you can upgrade it all by yourself. Years ago, I started a secret journal for the express purpose of upgrading my relationship. My husband was going through a tough time, and there was little I could do to help him. So I decided to try a 30 day experiment and write nice things about him every day. I would take 5-10 minutes to write something positive about my husband, usually 3 items I liked or appreciated about him. It was a great exercise. Every day, without him even knowing, I was focusing positive energy toward him. I noticed within a week he was starting to feel better and by the end of the month he even said "I've felt so much better this month!" It was then I told him what I'd done and he was very grateful. It worked so well, I kept up the practice for 2 years. So, even if you're alone in your desire to upgrade your relationship, you can still work wonders.

Now, even when we upgrade our relationships there will always be an ebb and flow. The NEW you introduce may become an old worn-out habit in a month. All we can do is accept the ebb and flow and when we feel we're entering a drought, it's time for another upgrade. I've upgraded my relationship so many times over the years and I'll continue to do so. And as that cheeky spirit baby not so subtly pointed out, I think it's time for another one.

It's Really About Self-Love
All of these frequency jumpers embody the broader subject of SELF-LOVE. Self-love is truly the one and only tool we need. EVER. Self-love is the cleanser and purifier, clearing out all the other things that are keeping us stuck and small. Self-love IS the vibration raiser. When we talk to ourselves in a positive way, that's self-love. When we embrace our emotions, no matter how uncomfortable they are, that's self-love. And every time we decide to upgrade our relationship we are also choosing to love ourselves. The more we learn to fully love ourselves every step of the way, the closer our souls come to home.

8

Physical Considerations

As I've said previously, when our vibration raises and our consciousness expands, our biology has no choice but to follow suit. And as I keep saying, this is a very organic process that happens automatically. What's actually happening is that as we remember the truth of who we are, our bodies return to their natural, pristine state.

And this is where it gets REALLY good, Sister. Our bodies, in their natural divine forms, DO NOT AGE. This means no stupid biological clock to worry about anymore. Disease and illness are also unnecessary as our bodies are able to self-correct and self-balance all of their own accord. But I'm getting ahead of myself. I'll talk more of the perks in the section "The Magic of a Limitless Life." In the meantime, just know Sister, our bodies ARE changing.

However, even though physical transformation happens automatically, I'm not going to lie and say it happens gracefully. Far from it!

WHAT ALL SPIRIT BABIES WANT THEIR MAMAS TO KNOW

As you know by now I'm a forerunner, meaning I'm among the first wave of people to go through this process. It's bound to be more drawn-out and messy for me. But even though the ones awakening behind the forerunners will have it easier, that doesn't mean it will be easy. There are some pesky little side effects to be aware of like...

<u>Pain</u>
When we shine our increasing light on our emotional body, all the repressed emotions come to the surface to be loved. Similarly, when our cells start lighting up, all the old cell memories from this lifetime and lifetimes past also come to the surface to be released. Everyone's process is unique, but everyone will be going through some uncomfortable physical restructuring.

What you'll discover along the way is that any ailment you can't cure, heal, or fix is really a stubborn, yet potent, "ascension symptom." The bad news is you can't cure it. The good news is it'll go away on its own. Eventually. Some ailments will leave overnight, some will stick around for weeks or even longer. Ascension symptoms can not be diagnosed. I've heard so many stories of people going to doctors for particular ascension symptoms and hearing that nothing is really wrong. In fact, both chronic fatigue syndrome and fibromyalgia are doctor-made-up terms for unexplainable "ascension symptoms." Some ailments are more stubborn than others, but they all will eventually go away on their own.

We should look at any pain we're experiencing as a past life trauma that is coming to the light to be healed. If it sticks around awhile, just picture it as something that needs the prolonged benefit of our light. Picture any pain as simply a sunbathing booboo. It's melding with our LIGHT until it becomes one with us. When it is wholed within us, it doesn't hurt anymore. There's nothing we need to do but trust and embrace the process. Easier said than done, but truly the only course of action.

Fatigue and Exhaustion

Exhaustion can also be a constant companion during our physical transformation. It makes sense since our bodies are undergoing TREMENDOUS rewiring. Often times the physical transformation demands so much energy that we have no energy left for anything else. This can be an extremely frustrating part of our journey, yet there is nothing we can do but honor it. Forerunners (myself included) have tried anything and everything to alleviate the exhaustion ~ supplements, diet changes, changes in activity, energy work, etc ~ but nothing helps. When our bodies are asking for more rest, the only thing we can do to truly help is rest. Period. It can be inconvenient and irritating, but we can comfort ourselves by understanding that AMAZING things are happening within us. We can even think of exhaustion as a primary emotion. There's nothing wrong with the exhaustion, in and of itself, but when we ignore it or resist it with judgment, it sticks around much longer until we freakin' cooperate already! Constant exhaustion has been one of my personal dragons to battle. I would get angry at it and feel victimized by it repeatedly. It was an awful loop I created for myself and it lasted for YEARS.

Nowadays if I feel extreme exhaustion I simply acknowledge it, honor it, and cheerlead my body for doing a great job. And then I'll have a movie marathon. Could be worse.

Weight Gain

Another unfortunate, and especially pesky physical side effect of our expanding consciousness is weight gain. Not everyone experiences this, but it is so prevalent among awakening people I'd be remiss not to mention it, even at the risk of scaring you off. (Seriously, if someone told me I'd gain weight without any conscious participation of my own, I may have skipped enlightenment altogether. True story.)

Years ago, I noticed this growing KNOWING that my body was about to go through a transformation. I didn't know what kind of transformation it would be, but I knew it was going to be GOOD. I didn't have a frame of reference for this knowing, and back then there little information about it. What I was starting to feel all those years ago was my lightbody coming on-line. What I didn't know was that I'd experience a very different and very uncomfortable physical transformation first.

Along with the privilege of experiencing debilitating migraines, chronic fatigue and fibromyalgia, I also had the honor of gaining twenty pounds and aging about a decade in the span of a couple of years. Good times.

What made my experience worse, especially in the beginning, was my RESISTANCE to it. Resistance = Suffering. I suffered through a lot of stuff that perhaps could have gone easier. I didn't have a clue of the higher purpose behind all this, so what I did was fight it. There was a lot of swearing at the universe.

The first thing I did when I seemingly gained weight overnight, was join a gym and start a diet. I'd been a personal trainer before having my first baby and I knew all the old formulas to get back into shape. The trouble was, they were truly OLD formulas and no longer worked. No matter how much I exercised or how little I ate, this ascension weight wouldn't budge. In fact I just gained more. Finally I started catching on that there was something more going on here than on just a physical level. So I quit the fucking gym and started eating again.

There was frustration in not being able to use food and exercise to lose weight, but there was also a certain feeling of freedom to it. I recalled what I was told during my "initiation"~ food and exercise will not matter in the higher dimensions. Obviously that was starting now. **I was beginning to understand that food, as well as no longer being a tool for nourishing my body, was also no longer a tool for controlling or manipulating my body.** I had to just sit with the weight and let my body do whatever it had to do. It WAS a freedom, even if a frustrating one.

Not everyone gains ascension weight but I had to. For many reasons. For one thing, my greatest fear since having an eating disorder in my teens was gaining weight. Weight gain (without any physical reason) was one of the dragons I had to fight. Understanding that my self-worth was not tied to my weight was a huge lesson in self-love for me.

Also, my body gained weight for the reasons of "protecting" itself as I started holding more light. As my intuition into other dimensions increased, the weight helped anchor and ground me into the Earth plane. Like postpartum weight, it's temporary. Granted it's lasted YEARS (dammit!), but I know it will go away on its own, just as it came on its own.

As of this writing, my body has FINALLY started shedding some of the extra density. Interestingly, just like it came on overnight, it seemed to come off overnight. This is a clear indicator that it's a different kind of weight, a different kind of density. Instead of a gradual, steady decline, which we've come to expect through diet and exercise, it comes off in large chunks and all at once. At least that's been my experience. All at once. Then nothing. All at once. Then nothing. It'll be interesting to see how the rest of our physical transformation transpires!

Our bodies go through a destruction phase before they are able to restructure and reconfigure. All past distortions come to the surface for releasing. As I've increased my light quotient, my body has had all sorts of lumps, bumps, wrinkles, and puckers come up. I feel like I'm wearing my dragons for all to see. And while it's not my preference to display my body's destructive phase, I've absolutely learned to love myself through it. My self-worth is NOT tied to my body in any way, shape, or form. Talk about freedom, Sister!

Weight fluctuations can also go the other way. I heard from a second-waver recently (the group waking up behind the forerunners) who LOST extra weight while doing her shadow work. Frankly, that order makes MUCH more sense to me, and I would wish that for anyone who desires it. But I've also come to look at extra weight very differently and without judgment. If I see someone gain a lot of weight in a short amount of time, I'm EXCITED for them. I know they are in a pivotal part of their spiritual journey, doing really important work, and ultimately getting ready for an AMAZING transformation.

Food Matters, Until It Doesn't
It's easy to read about the pain, fatigue, and weight gain associated with awakening and perhaps think a change in diet can alleviate all of it. I know many forerunners who have spent a lot of time tinkering with food and exercise and supplements (myself included) in the hopes of helping/controlling/manipulating our bodies. As you've read, nothing worked for me. And in the long run, none of these outside sources of "help" will work for anyone. Many forerunners may have experienced a brief reprieve from symptoms while trying something new only to wind up in the same place or worse. Ultimately our bodies have the last say, and they're telling us (if we listen closely enough) that they can handle this on their own, thank you very much.

Pain, fatigue, and weight gain are not indications that something is WRONG with our bodies. If we have to go to the doctor to find that out, fine. Eventually we'll understand that all the symptoms we experience during awakening are simply indications of our spiritual, emotional, and physical transformation. The feelings associated with the symptoms, whether it's frustration, anger, or victimization are the dragons we're fighting along the way. When we're able to work through them, we clear so much ick from our spiritual self. Truly, SO MUCH is happening on so many levels.

The less we resist the aches and pains, and the more we can cheerlead our bodies for doing amazing, heroic work, the easier and faster our transformation will be. Our bodies know exactly what they're doing, we just need to be on board and be patient with them.

Our bodies have so much wisdom and they'll tell us what they need. Much like the suggestions in the section "The Best Pregnancy Advice Ever," we should listen closely to our bodies to see what they want to eat, what they don't want to eat, how they want to move, and how much they need to rest. We may find that our taste buds are changing, as well as our preferences. Personally, I went from eating chocolate every day to not being able to handle the taste of any kind of sweet for years. I couldn't even eat fruit. This was not a voluntary change and many times I would miss the ability to eat a cookie or ice cream or even a grape! But it was clear that my body did not want those foods and it was impossible to ignore. Also impossible to ignore were the times my body needed all kinds of salt. It all balances out eventually.

The bottom line: we need to LISTEN to our bodies. We can try vegan, we can try raw, or we can try an all protein diet. There is plenty of new age advice out there that will tell us exactly what to eat. But all these diets are still based on judgment. Healthy foods = good. Unhealthy foods = bad. Even calling something healthy or unhealthy is a judgment. One of the biggest parts of the journey is releasing judgment...of ALL things, including food.

For awhile food will matter to many of us during our transformation, so we should do what feels good at the time, allowing ourselves to change as our bodies need. Ultimately though, when we're done tinkering with the diets and can eat solely from a place of LOVE, we will discover that food truly doesn't matter anymore.

The time is coming very soon for all us when food is eaten only for pleasure, joy, and celebration. Our bodies will be fueled only by the source of our own LOVE and no matter what we eat or don't eat, our bodies will be perfectly sustained. Now doesn't that sound like the perfect meal?

9

Dark Night of the Soul

I don't want to give you more bad news, but the journey to bliss is not exactly blissful. (At any point that my words make you want to bow out of this whole crazy thing, jump ahead and read the next chapter so you can see why we're doing all of this to begin with.) You've probably heard the term "dark night of the soul," as it's becoming a far more common term the more people experience it.

The first thing I have to say about the dark night of the soul is that it's a misnomer. If ONLY it was one night. It's not one night. And it's not even a continuous stretch of time. I've mentioned that I experienced a three year dark night of the soul, but it wasn't a constant three year darkness. It was a darkness interspersed with light and fullness. The dark night of the soul is actually a vacillation between days of flow, where everything is wonderful and days where everything sucks and you just want to END IT ALREADY!

What we're actually experiencing is the neutralization of polarity. We are moving beyond judgment of "good or bad," and "right or wrong." We are releasing any and all ideas that keep us in separation consciousness. Our mind is being rewired and we are making a break from the matrix that keeps us in fear and limitation. We are also shedding our old worn-out identities in order to become a fresh, blank slate. And it can hurt like hell. No one said change was easy.

I've experienced so many "dark nights of the soul" throughout the years, as has my enlightened husband, that we simply just call it "the darkness." Some days we're in the darkness, some days we are in the light. And the interesting thing about both the light and the dark, is that spiritual amnesia accompanies them. When we're in the dark, it feels like we've been there forever! When we're in the light, we're sure we've always been in the light! When we're in the light, we don't understand how we can be kept down by the darkness. When we're in the darkness, we're sure we'll never see the light again. Both are all encompassing experiences.

I've also come to believe that there are two kinds of darkness. There's one that is really stagnation, and we're able to shift out of it by doing something different or uplifting, even if just by changing our perspective. Then there's the darkness that is truly unrelenting. We can't shift out of it no matter how hard we try, no matter what we do. This is the darkness we have to sit in and just love ourselves through, while waiting for it to pass. I've had many days of darkness where I've had to go hide in my room so I don't scream at everyone. Those are the days it's hard for even me to be around myself. I'd often get the inner vision of me rocking in a dark corner silently whispering "I love myself" repeatedly as the dragons warred around me. Those are the days that suck.

And we'll all go through them to some extent. The key, as with everything, is non-resistance. Resisting the darkness causes suffering and lord knows we don't need that on top of everything else. Talking to ourselves lovingly while we experience the darkness is a VERY high vibrational thing to do. I've said to myself often "This is hard and it hurts, but you're doing a great job." Sometimes I just binge watch movies and shut the fuck up. We need to do whatever we can to just let the darkness pass through us without getting angry at ourselves or telling ourselves we're doing something wrong.

Because the darkness is actually doing VERY important work. It's like a scouring brush on all the darkest, deepest, most stuck ickiness. We don't have to examine it or understand it, we have to just allow ourselves to be cleansed. After each dark episode there's always a frequency jump.

At first, the shift from light days to dark days will feel like a huge pendulum swing ~ days of darkness followed by days of peace (though during the most intense time, the dark days FAR outweigh the days of peace). Then as duality starts to settle into divine neutrality (nonjudgment) things to start to balance out. As our vibration increases, the swings become less and less pronounced. We can have a dark moment immediately followed by a moment of peace.

Even though I say I'm now out of the "dark night of the soul," I still have moments of darkness. But they're only moments. And without an attachment to them, the moments of peace are not far behind. Now the days of peace are the norm. What used to be days or weeks of darkness, is just a moment. And whew! What a relief!

Absolutely EVERYTHING is getting rewired within us during the dark night of the soul. We'll find that our interests change, our passions wane, our relationships drift, our priorities change. Often times we'll just feel like an empty shell. It's all appropriate and exactly as it should be. It's the unlearning of everything, including who we thought we were and what we thought our purpose was, so we can eventually rediscover ourselves in a brand new way we can't even imagine from our current vantage point. Suffice to say, when this whole process is over, we'll be more US than we ever were before. A brand new expanded, limitless, fearless, and wildly creative higher version of ourselves.

We'll make it through the dark night of the soul. And we'll be better than ever. It's inevitable.

10
Working With The New Energy

As our consciousness expands new energy becomes available to us. And it works very differently than the old energy. There can be some frustration with this because there is a learning curve as we transition between energy systems. I've banged my head against many a wall when trying to make something new happen with old tools. It just doesn't work. It's difficult to define because the new energy responds uniquely to each person wielding it.

What I can say about the new energy is that it doesn't work linearly. Linear time is a construct of the old energy. In the new energy, we'll notice our relationship with time changing. We'll forget what day it is, what month it is, and even what season we're in. It's not because we're becoming forgetful, it's because linear time is dissolving.

We'll even discover we can bend time. If I find myself running late for something, instead of rushing I'll slow down, take a deep breath, and affirm "I'll get there exactly when I'm supposed to." And I'm never late.

Ever. Even if I show up after the time I'm supposed to, I'll still be the first one there. My boys often joke with me saying "Even when you're late, you're early." So, don't expect things to happen linearly. There's a lot of freedom in that. It means things don't have to change slowly and steadily over time anymore. There are quantum leaps available to us in the new energy. We should really take that to heart, because it means that even if change looks so far off from where we're standing at the moment, the truth is, now dramatic change can happen in an instant. Amen to that!

Forcing, efforting, or trying also doesn't work in the new energy. We can no longer make things happen by the sheer force of our will. This is also another thing that can be intensely frustrating until we learn that things can happen MUCH easier in the new energy.

The new energy is one of effortlessness. The only rule that comes with it is: **if it's not effortless, don't do it.** In the new energy there's a lot less doing and a lot more trusting. Instead of forcing, we have to trust that when we're meant to do something, the path will open up wide for us when the time is right.

And when it is time for us to do something we'll experience a compulsion that we just can't ignore. This compulsion is "inspired action." When it's time to do something, we can't possibly stop ourselves. If we try to talk ourselves out of the compulsion, it will just continue to get stronger until ignoring it becomes absolute torture (I speak from experience). The compulsion toward inspired action then leads us to an effortlessness of joyful creation. It's really quite wonderful!

The birthing of this book was a new energy creation. For a couple of years writing this book has been in the back of my mind, but I just couldn't force myself to do it. That's because it simply wasn't time yet. Not too long ago I had a dream that showed me it was time to write, and I was shown where I should go to do it ~ my Grandma's old beach in Maine. I woke up EXCITED that it was finally time to get this book out of me, and then summoned my long-passed Grandma to help make it happen. Soon after, in flooded a whole host of support from all the realms. I received surprise money from a friend and sold more spirit baby readings than usual. My parents found me a beach house to rent just a few doors down from my Grandma's old place (and I was treated to the synchronicity that the woman who owns it has the same name as my Grandma). All other details just fell into place. All I had to do was show up. Writing the book itself has also been an effortless and joyful process that's only taken me five days to get on paper. It's been an absolutely wonderful experience in every way. That's the way of the new energy.

The new energy will lead us to our dreams, or more accurately, we'll use the new energy to create our dreams. But everyone has to get to know the new energy in their own unique way. **It responds to our intentions and affirmations and what we believe.** It's like our very own sparkly magic wand. Wield it wisely, Sister!

The Magic of a Limitless Life
It's hard to fully describe the magic that our lives will become when we've reached a high enough vibration to reunite with our souls, because it's a completely different existence than what we're experiencing now. It's not like our lives now with just a little more money, a little more joy, a little more passion. It's a complete internal overhaul that takes our life experience to an entirely different level. The things we thought were impossible all at once become inevitable.

Due to my three week soul immersion all those years ago, and my growing intuition ever since, I'm able to see some of the amazingness that we'll become. Though I bet there's so much more that I can't even imagine yet.

How it Feels
Just as magical as the things we'll be gaining in our limitless lives, are the things we'll be losing. We won't feel fear anymore, and with that

we won't feel the need to keep ourselves constantly safe and protected. Imagine all the energy just that alone frees up! The majority of our human life up until now has circulated around doing things to keep us safe and protected. Indeed our very existence has been based on fear. That is a HUGE thing we'll be leaving behind.

Fear is a repellent, keeping away the very things that we're all entitled to as our birthright. Fear of not having enough money, repels money. Fear of not having health, repels health. And it's all based on lies. Our natural divine state is one of self-sustaining abundance, health, creativity, joy, youth, and love. All of these things have been stripped away from us (as part of our agreement to experience this limited vibration) and then sold back to us from outside sources.

Now we are waking up and claiming what is rightfully ours. Fear is the lie and it won't have a hold on us anymore. What will replace fear will be expansive feelings of interest, joy, and celebration.

We'll know we can create whatever we wish and understand that all the resources we need will come to us.

We'll live in complete trust that everything we need will show up exactly when it's supposed to.

We'll feel such an IMMERSION in life, that everything feels comfortable and intimate.

We'll feel HOME no matter where we are.

There will be a confidence and a levity in all our actions and interactions.

WHAT ALL SPIRIT BABIES WANT THEIR MAMAS TO KNOW

We will feel like a higher version of ourselves and be able to see the higher versions of everyone else, even if they are not acting from that higher place.

We will be unable to be drawn into drama, unless we want to simply for entertainment reasons, and then it will just feel fun.

We will laugh so much more and discover a playfulness that perhaps we've never experienced before. We also may find that, damn, we are freakin' funny!

These are many of things we'll FEEL when we're in our limitless state but there's also many wonderful things we can expect from our lightbodies. Our bodies will automatically transform to reflect our higher vibration, and with that come certain upgrades.

<u>How It Looks</u>
Our bodies will no longer be something we have to take care of. They will become their own self-sustainable, self-correcting, self-harmonizing vessels. Perhaps you would think that would diminish our relationship with our bodies, but the opposite is true. Instead of having to spend so much time taking care of our bodies' needs, we will now be free to experience our bodies in new and exciting ways. We'll no longer have to use food as nourishment nor worry about keeping our bodies fit through exercise. We will eat for pleasure and move for joy. Period. And our body will take care of it's own perfect, pristine form. Hallelujah!

We'll be able to self-regulate our body temperature, never worrying about being too hot or cold.

We'll discover new and amazing abilities, gifts, and talents.

Our bodies will also no longer age nor experience illness and disease. THIS is a big one. Especially in relation to pregnancy, Sister. Let's explore this a little more...

Limitless Pregnancy and Birth

With a self-sustaining, self-harmonizing body that doesn't age we will never have to worry about being "too old" to have a baby. Our bodies will not be the fragile vessels they are viewed as now, and the term "high-risk-pregnancy" will cease to exist. Our bodies will be able to easily conceive and carry our babies.

And here's a good one. Four words: No more morning sickness! That speaks for itself.

Unplanned pregnancies will also be a thing of the past, replaced with "conscious conception." Bringing in a baby will be a conscious choice between partners, and when the time feels right we will invite the baby in. By then our intuition will be honed and prebirth communication with our spirit babies will be as easy as calling them on the phone.

With conscious conception we'll never have to worry about getting pregnant without our consent. And man, I just LOVE that idea! No more birth control!

Pregnancy will be easy and beautiful, as will be carrying to full term.

Birth will be empowered, sacred, peak experiences for all involved. The way it should be.

Am I Bat-Shit Crazy?

That would be a fair question. But these are not just lofty ideas, Sister. It's already happening. And thankfully we don't have to wait for our souls to be fully reunited with us before we start to experience many of these perks. I'm experiencing a fair amount of them already and I know many others are too. I'll share some with you.

- My body has become much less dependent upon food as a fuel source. My interest in food had waned considerably as this takes place. I have little need or interest in eating. This is true for many other forerunners I know as well. I continue to eat just because it's a habit, but I skip many meals and only eat when I truly have to or want to. Now, I could eat a lot if I really wanted to. I could eat a whole buffet of food and know my body could self-balance, but during this part of my transition I'm simply not interested. Any food I do eat must be food prepared and infused with LOVE, or I'd rather just go without. As of this writing, I'm either not eating, eating only food prepared with love, or eating food that delights my inner child. If it's not pleasurable food, I'll just skip it altogether.
- I'm able to regulate my body temperature on command. I discovered I could do this while venturing out on a walk in the woods in the winter without enough layers. Instead of turning back for a heavy coat, I simply affirmed to my body that I was warm and comfortable. And I was. I've now been doing this for years.
- I'm finally experiencing more and more days of limitless flow. This means I'm feeling those feelings of being home wherever I am, a levity in all my interactions, and feelings of being immersed in life. It's so beautiful and so full and maybe, just maybe, it's becoming permanent.
- I'm experiencing amazing telepathic interactions with animals as my intuition expands.
- I've also experienced miracles twice this year of being able to jump timelines when I was experiencing something I didn't want to experience. The first time was when my father was in the hospital dying very rapidly from a rare tick-borne disease. When I talked to him on the phone I knew he was dying, and

moreover, so did he. I couldn't stop shaking afterwards, so I went into the woods to find my center. While in the woods I tapped into my limitlessness and DECIDED very firmly what I was going to experience. I knew there were infinite timelines and infinite possibilities available, so I chose the one I wanted to experience ~ the one where my Dad not only lived through this experience, but became even healthier. I scripted it as I walked, saying I'd get a phone call the next day telling me he would be okay. As I walked out of the woods, I left it up to my soul to orchestrate. The next day I DID get that phone call. He'd been transferred to another hospital that knew exactly how to treat his rare illness, and he seemed to be surrounded by angelic staff. He went home just days later. Today my Dad is the healthiest he's been in years.

This taught me so much about the power we have to choose our experiences. I knew I didn't "heal" my Dad, I simply chose the timeline I wanted to engage with. And thankfully, this knowledge came in handy a few months later when my husband, who was cycling with two of his friends on an overnight trip, was hit by a truck. I was out with my boys when I noticed I'd missed a text from my husband that simply said "Call." I knew right away something terrible had happened. He'd texted during the time he was to be riding, and the vagueness of the message made me wonder if perhaps one of his friends had texted me because something happened to him. Before I called him back, I centered myself and said out loud "I choose the timeline where my husband is okay."

And although my husband had hit the truck head on while on his bike, and had a black-eye and stitches in his knee, he WAS okay. Miraculously. His two friends suffered far more extensive injuries and would need months and months to recover, but my husband, who hit the truck most directly, was able to walk away. No one could explain it or understand it. It was another miracle.

WHAT ALL SPIRIT BABIES WANT THEIR MAMAS TO KNOW

Granted these aren't exactly the circumstances I want to experience when commanding forth miracles, but along our path of transformation it's important we understand that we can handle anything life throws at us, and we do have the choice AND power to command a best-case-scenario.

Although the information in this section may seem a bit fringe and so far off in the future, the truth is it's so much closer than we think. The more and more people that awaken (and awakening is inevitable), the more accelerated change we'll experience.

We Don't Have to Wait
When masses of people begin to awaken, change happens at a faster rate ~ sort of like a tidal wave. However, we don't have to wait for everyone else to wake up before we can get to the good stuff. It's the transformation of the individual that transforms the world.

Transformation is the very thing we came to experience in this lifetime ~ the transformation from human to divine human. As our generation wakes up to remembering the truth of our divinity, our children will come in remembering theirs. When we remember our own limitlessness, we allow our children to keep their own. Instead of forgetting our origins upon birth, the new children will preserve theirs. When we awaken and remember, it is a gift to us and to our children.

The spirit babies are VERY grateful to this current generation of parents. They know the difficult road we've chosen, as we destructively unlearn everything that's come before us to courageously build something new that we can't even yet fathom. We are leaving behind all that is comfortable and familiar to become grander versions of ourselves, so in turn our children can be grander versions of themselves.

It can be a difficult and daunting task, even in its brilliance, which is why the spirit baby realm is so invested in aiding us any way they can.

We evolve through love, for love, and by love. In every moment we have a choice to make between fear and love. In every moment there is an invitation to limit ourselves or to choose limitlessness. Fear limits us, love expands us. When faced with a choice, ask yourself which reality will serve you?

We may not be able to always choose how we feel, but we can always choose to honor how we feel. If we're tired and exhausted, we can speak lovingly to our body and give it the rest it needs. If we're angry, we can honor the anger for the message it brings us, knowing it's lovingly serving us. If we're frustrated and stuck, we can sit lovingly with it and know an answer will come.

LOVE is the fast-track. LOVE is the magic pill. LOVING ourselves unconditionally through our transformation is the easiest way ~ the ONLY way.

When we love ourselves enough, the journey becomes joyful. I can honestly say I'm now in a joyful part of my awakening journey. I'm joyful as I discover the expansiveness of myself as a limitless expression of perfect love. In each moment I know I can use love as my very own super-power and magic wand. It's amazing, miraculous and extremely fulfilling. And I know it's only the very tip of the iceberg.

There's so much more to explore and remember. So much more than what is in these pages or our imaginations. It's truly a journey of discovery that we are all on together ~ you, me, our children and our future children. We're discovering what a new world looks like based on the limitlessness of LOVE. Even if we can't fully imagine it, we know it can only be beautiful.

It's not that far away. Don't forget, in the new energy linear time doesn't exist. **What seems so far away now could literally be here within the next breath.** It's in you at this very moment ~ and your spirit baby is helping you remember.

Part Three

11

Your Spirit Baby Reading

The best way for me to sum up all the wisdom from the spirit baby realm is to end this book with a reading. The type of reading I do is a bit different than most. It's not a "predict-the-future" kind of reading, it's more of a life coaching session from the perspective of the spirit baby. It shows the highest path and then invites the mama to step into it. **These words are meant for you.** Feel the energy of your spirit baby engulfing you as you read and know it's a promise from your future child. Take a deep breath, expand your perception, and receive the wisdom and love from your baby....

Okay, Dear Sister, the first thing your spirit baby wants you to know is that if you're yearning for a baby, that baby is also yearning for you. The desire for a baby is never a one-way street. If you want a baby, then that baby also wants to come to you. Often times it's the baby's desire to come Earthside that precipitates the mother's yearning for a baby in the first place. Just your interest alone in having a baby, tells me right away that there is a spirit baby (or babies) in your energetic field planning on coming in. Rest assured your spirit baby is here with you (in my perception floating in an energetic orb around your head) and you are indeed meant to be a mama.

But you have a special role. You're not meant to be "just" a mama, you're meant to be a New Earth mama. Your spirit baby carries a very high vibration, meaning he or she vibrates to the frequency of unconditional love. This is the frequency needed to build the New Earth. As such, it's part of your role to be a quick-study in raising your vibration to meet that of your baby.

When parents are of a different vibration to the new children coming in, much of their relationship is spent breaking down old limits, barriers, and blocks. It can be a challenging relationship when we're not vibrationally resonant. However when we're able to meet our children at their own very high vibration, we can partner together joyfully as we create and explore the new. It's a much more harmonious experience and one that your baby is inviting you to.

It's important to your spirit baby that you understand that any difficulties you've experienced in life doesn't mean you've done something wrong. Even though it can often be a stressful, and frustrating journey, it's a journey you agreed to experience as part of your soul contract. Difficulties of any kind serve you for higher reasons ~ either of karmic clearing from past lifetimes or of soul growth in this lifetime. Often both are happening at the same time.

Know that all your challenges have helped you grow in leaps and bounds more than any easy path you could have taken, which is why it's sometimes been so intense. Instead of feeling like a victim when you experience something challenging, your spirit baby says you should feel like a victor ~ for you have fulfilled your soul contract beautifully.

WHAT ALL SPIRIT BABIES WANT THEIR MAMAS TO KNOW

So many times it's easy to get caught up in doing the "right" things, eating the "right" things, acting the "right" way, having the "right" thoughts and even being the "right" age in order to "deserve" a baby. However **your spirit baby is telling you that having your heart's desires is your birthright**! What you want most in life is not something you have to earn or deserve, it is your birthright ~ and this includes everything, even your baby. Difficulties and challenges along the way have nothing to do with doing things wrong or not being good enough in any way. There should be no guilt or judgment attached to why things take longer than you want. All is unfolding as it should and all for higher reasons that you must trust.

The journey of this particular lifetime is a vibrational one. Your vibration has increased exponentially along the way and you're about to take a major quantum leap. Your spirit baby also wants to point out that as your consciousness expands, your biology has no choice but to catch up. All of us are in the midst of a grand evolutionary change, where not only our minds are being rewired into higher understandings, our bodies are also coming on-line in new ways. With your new biology, silly old out-dated theories (read: limited thinking) don't apply anymore. You may find that as your biology returns to a natural pristine state, new abilities open up and places where your biology used to limit you are completely overhauled and reworked.

When faced with a decision and you don't know how to proceed, know that many new options are now opening for you. Paths that were entirely appropriate in the old world will still be appropriate for some time during the transitioning of worlds, but new choices you'd never considered before will now appear within your view. And you get to decide which way to go at every turn. Feel into your timelines and possibilities and see which one brings the most joy and feeling of expansiveness. Mentally try on the many options and then feel into what option resonates highest with you, then choose to align with that. **You can't get it wrong.**

And while you can't control Divine Timing (trust me, I've tried many times over to no avail) know that the frustrating part of your journey can now come to an end, while an easier, more joyful journey now begins ~ a journey with your spirit baby as a full partner, guide, and cheerleader.

Your spirit baby is asking you to trust in Divine Timing, as it always brings us something better than we could have personally planned ourselves. Look at any delays you've experienced as protection ~ protection against anything less than your truest heart's desires and your highest soul purpose. It's time to let go of any previous agenda, timetable or expectation and allow your soul to be in the driver's seat.

Be sure to talk to your spirit baby, because he or she is here already communicating with you. Look for the signs and acknowledge them when they come. Listen to your dreams and write them down. Important messages are given in dreams. Keep a journal to have ongoing conversations with your baby. You'll be surprised by how much information you'll get. And quiet your mind in meditation to listen to the small still voice of wisdom within. You already know exactly what you need.

Keep an eye out for a totem ~ your spirit baby will be sending you one. It will be an animal or natural object that is obvious and/or repetitive. Know that this totem is your power animal and a promise from your spirit baby that you will get your heart's desires.

By now I hope you're feeling a lightening of the spirit. You're following your soul contract to the letter, you've endured the difficulties and challenges in your life for higher reasons of the soul, you've done absolutely nothing wrong, and you're now breaking through old limits and fears. The suffering part of your journey is now over and you're free to begin anew.

What should you do with this freed-up energy? Why, explore your expanding vibration, of course! (And here come some activations,

WHAT ALL SPIRIT BABIES WANT THEIR MAMAS TO KNOW

Sister, hold onto your hat...) You can now stop trying to make things happen and start discovering yourself in a new way. Your spirit baby wants you to know that you are FREE. You're more free now than you've ever been. If you've been pre-occupied, distracted, and obsessed with things turning out a certain way, know that it is time to truly let go and release. Wipe your mind of the doubt, the frustration, the impatience. Those feelings were appropriate before, but they are not appropriate now. For you are FREE. You are free to FEEL THE KNOWING in your heart. You are free to have whatever you truly want in your life ~ people, experiences, things, talents, gifts. You are FREE to have all your heart's desires. Know this.

With the knowledge of your freedom come different ways of being. Imagine that you've been in a cage this whole time, and the door has now been opened. That is exactly what has happened ~ and yet, most people get so used to the cage that they don't even see the open door or know what to do with it, so they just sit there, not knowing a whole new world has opened up.

A new world, no matter how wonderful, can be scary at first because it's so unfamiliar. We've been taught to be afraid of the unfamiliar, so again we sit in our uncomfortable cage because it's familiar. Take the first step and walk out of that damn cage. Be brave, Dear Sister, and walk into the unknown. Allow yourself to feel disorientated and confused at first. Know that if you keep taking steps you'll easily learn the ways of your new world. It won't take long. Your spirit baby and your soul are guiding you. **Allow yourself to be led. Allow yourself to be cradled. Allow it to unfold beautifully before you. Just take that first step out of your cage.**

You'll know you're ready to step out of your cage when you're ready to try new things. This is where your soul really starts to shine. There are things your soul came here to experience, and NOW is the time. Put your hand to heart, Dear Sister, and listen to the desires of your soul that have been whispering in your ear since your childhood. Children are innately in touch with their souls, until they're taught not to be, and then they forget. It's time to remember why you came here and what you wanted to experience. Your spirit baby wants this FOR you. Your spirit baby wants you to be happy. Happy mamas make happy babies. REMEMBER.

Follow the JOY. Joy is the true north on your new world compass. If an idea or an experience elicits a joyful response from you, you'll know that your soul has choreographed it and you should follow it. You'll find that being joyful actually takes a lot less energy than suffering. But it will take practice until joy becomes your default. **Keep doing new things, have new thoughts, create new patterns, change your daily routine around.** Don't try to recreate the patterns from your small caged-in life. Joy is BIG and without limits. You are limitless now. Follow your limitless joy.

Talk to yourself like you believe in yourself. This again take practice until it becomes a default but it feels so much better. When you hear that sad voice in your head say "I'm not good enough. This is taking too long. What am I doing wrong?" affirm instead "I'll have what I need when the time is right. I trust myself." Do this with any negative self talk ~ just redirect it as if you BELIEVE you're free, and as if you BELIEVE that you're about to get exactly what you want. Repeat. Repeat. Repeat.

Dedicate yourself to YOURSELF! Dedicate yourself to living freely and joyfully! Dedicate yourself to having exactly what you want because you KNOW you deserve it! Dedicate yourself to exquisite pleasure! To delirious happiness! To sensual food! To hot sex! To saying YES when you want to and saying NO when you don't want to! Dedicate yourself to all things decadent and luxurious and beautiful. PLEASURE and JOY are our birthrights and THAT'S what we came here to experience. This is what your spirit baby is coming to experience. We are here to be FULLY ourselves, in our own unique way ~ to play, to laugh, to love.

WHAT ALL SPIRIT BABIES WANT THEIR MAMAS TO KNOW

Be you ~ the BIG you ~ and live the life you've always dreamed. There is nothing you can't do. So DO IT. And know that your spirit baby is cheering for you the whole way...

The Beginning.

FAQ's

Q: **I've been trying to conceive for 3 years. I understand that this is all part of my vibrational journey, but does that mean I won't have my baby until I'm fully integrated with my soul?**

A: Absolutely not. Spirit babies can act as catalysts for their parents' spiritual awakening, but that doesn't mean we have to complete the journey before they come to us. Remember, we don't have to earn our babies. There is no true ending to our journeys. Our babies can come at any time during it.

Q: **What happens if I'm expanding my consciousness but my husband is not? Will I have to leave him behind?**

A: While many relationships in our lives will change and drift as we go through our transformation, this doesn't have to be the case with our significant others. When we start raising our vibration, the loved ones around us benefit as well. It can often in turn spark their own awakening. Everyone will go through their own transformation within their own time. Just keep loving him the best you can, honor his path, and his timing.

Q. **Will my aborted baby come back? I wasn't ready back then but I am now. Is she mad at me about that?**

A: Spirit babies don't share the judgment about abortion that we do as humans. Your baby knew that your past abortion was something you both agreed to experience together for higher reasons. She would never be angry at you for fulfilling your part of your soul contract. And if you're feeling the desire for her to come back, you can be sure that she is also feeling the desire to return to you. All is well and you'll both have a higher frequency of relationship this time around. There is no need for guilt or regret. It all played out as it should.

Q: **I've been sensing a spirit baby around me for a few months now but I'm not ready to invite her in. Is it okay if I ask her to wait or will she get impatient and go to someone else?**

A. Often babies come before conception to help prepare the mother for their arrival. Be open to her messages and then talk with her about when it would be best for her to come. This is a great opportunity to really establish a dialog and partnership with your baby. If you're not feeling ready for her but definitely want her, then the timing is most likely not right for her either. There's simply some preparations to make that she'd like your help with. Write in a journal any insights you receive.

Q: **I've been ttc for 4 years now with no luck. I know my biology is changing but I honestly don't know if I can wait for it to catch up. I want to be a mother now. Is it okay to explore other options like IVF or adoption? Will I miss my spirit baby if I choose an alternative method and get another baby instead?**

A: We can't miss our spirit babies. It's just not possible. Your spirit baby knows exactly what way he or she is coming to you. If you're feeling a strong pull to try other methods then you should explore those. Your spirit baby may very well be leading you to those areas. If a decision to explore IVF or adoption feels expansive and brings you relief then that's a good indication you're on the highest path. No matter what you decide, you can't get it wrong. You can't miss your spirit baby.

Q: **I'm ready for my spirit baby to come, but my husband is not. Will my baby still come even if his father is reluctant?**

WHAT ALL SPIRIT BABIES WANT THEIR MAMAS TO KNOW

A: While ideally we would consciously invite babies in when both parents are ready, and that's the future we're headed for, it's not entirely possible to create those conditions right now in every circumstance. And with no disrespect to our beloved men, it's usually the women who are more intuitively linked to the baby and the timing of it all. While we shouldn't go about tricking our men into getting us pregnant, babies can and do come through even with reluctant fathers. Sometimes the fathers just need a little push ~ and if that's the case, it's best to put our spirit babies to the task. Ask your baby to give your husband a dream or sign if it's in the best interests for all involved. Spirit babies can be very persuasive and when they're supposed to come in, they will. The higher version/vibration of reality ~ the one that serves everyone ~ will always prevail.

Q: I have four sons and while I really don't want any more children, I feel a spirit baby girl around me sometimes and it makes me yearn for her. I know my husband doesn't want more children and frankly, our marriage couldn't take the strain. My family right now is the most important thing to me. Is it appropriate for me to ask the spirit baby to go to someone else? I don't want to hurt her feelings. I've also always wanted a daughter and don't want to feel like I'm missing out.

A. It's entirely appropriate to tell the baby that while you love her you're just not able to take her on right now. Drawing boundaries like that can be an act of self-love, so honor it and your baby will too. Her feelings won't be hurt as they are not attached to certain outcomes as we are. She'll be able to fulfill her soul contract in other ways, spirit babies are very resourceful. And you also can't miss out. If there is some benefit to her energy you can ask to experience it in a different way. We may never know how it plays out but we just have to trust that everything is unfolding as it should. Our preferences absolutely matter. We don't have to sacrifice our own well-being for others anymore. Spirit babies often come in to teach us that very thing. You can also ask for your yearning for a daughter to go away. The yearning is often a reflection of the spirit baby's desire to come in. Once you say that's not going to happen, then you'll also notice that the yearning will dissipate. Wanting to enjoy your family the way it is now is also a very beautiful choice.

Q: I had a horrible birth experience followed by postpartum depression and I so worry about the effects it's had on my sweet boy baby, as it's taken me awhile to be able to bond with him. I'm worried I've ruined my baby straight from the get-go. Is this also something that was in our spiritual contracts to experience together?

A: First off, let me assure your that your baby knew what the birth experience and newborn period would entail. As you've said this was indeed part of your spiritual contract to experience together. And thankfully, the babies coming in carry such a high vibration they are much more self-possessed. They know exactly who they are and why they came here. Your baby knows that his arrival was an agent to your own karmic clearing, and he has not taken on any baggage as you go through this. We can't "ruin" our children anymore. He is just fine and will continue to be as you work through this.

Your birth experience most likely sparked a past life trauma which you are now working through karmically. Though it is a terribly difficult thing to go through, know that you are clearing lifetimes worth of stuff during this time. Many women who go through postpartum depression have to do something that they're not particularly good at: ask for help. Surround yourself with as much support as you can and get all the help you need. This is your time to be supported and cared for. Look at your postpartum depression as spiritual fast-tracking. You'll emerge from this brighter and with more clarity than ever. There are many gifts in this, so open yourself to them. And truly allow yourself to be supported in every way.

Q: Will my kids have to go through an awakening process too? I have a teenager, a 9 year old and a toddler. Or is their consciousness already high enough?

WHAT ALL SPIRIT BABIES WANT THEIR MAMAS TO KNOW

A: It is possible that some of the older kids who are here now may have some karma to work through even if they are of a high vibration. If they do, it will be much easier than the awakening process we're going through right now. However, the best thing we can do for our children is to raise our own vibration. When we're able to embody a higher frequency, our children benefit and are able follow suit. It's almost like they're waiting for us to light up before they fully light up themselves. As much as it's natural to worry about the spiritual journeys of our loved ones, the best thing (and only thing) we can do is work on ourselves. We'll notice that when we start to take on more light, everything and everyone around does as well.

Q: I believe I must be going through my dark night of the soul. I've lost interest in all my hobbies and I have no energy or enthusiasm for anything. I have two wonderful children and I feel like I'm missing out on their childhoods because I just can't engage with them like I want. I feel like my awakening journey is ruining my kids. Or at least ruining my enjoyment of them. Help?

A. This issue is near and dear to my own heart, as I've been there. For a long time this issue plagued me in the forms of anger, frustration and guilt. It took me a while to understand that this was simply another vehicle being used in order for me to transcend those feelings. Dragons in a different disguise. Understanding this helped. What also helped me was understanding that my kids knew EXACTLY what they were getting into when they decided to choose me as their mother. They knew there would be a long period of time where I had to rest more than usual and where I wouldn't be entirely present. They knew this and factored it into what they wanted to experience. Your children knew this too. It's been divinely orchestrated by all of you. It's all in perfect order.

And the last thing that helped me was the understanding that on the other side of this, I would be the mother I always wanted to be...and BETTER. As we raise our frequency and expand our consciousness, we are able to be mothers in a NEW way. Not only are we engaged with our children, we are immersed in them. It becomes an entirely different experience of parenting, where every breath is precious and every day an adventure to be explored. I can assure you from where I sit that you are not missing out on anything. In fact, you're about to celebrate motherhood and your children in beautiful new ways that you can't even yet imagine...

About the Author

I'm a bad-ass agent of change and warrior of LOVE. I use my intuitive abilities to communicate with the spirit baby realm, to talk to animals, and to bring in messages from the new world. I'm married to my soulmate and homeschool my three magical boys. We have three furry kitties and one big fluffy dog.

If you like me in print, you'll love me in video. Visit my website http://lovefrombaby.com for boatloads more info on spirit babies, pre-birth communication, awakening, and the new world.

Thank You

To my loved ones who supported this endeavor:

My dear friend, Val, for your generosity and love.

My parents, who found me the beach rental in which to write and who came to nurse me when I had a migraine. You've always been my biggest cheerleaders.

My soul sisters and fellow forerunners, Natalia, Carrie, and LJ. I would have never made it through this crazy-ass journey without all of you.

The Unseen Loved Ones, my Grandma, the Spirit Baby Realm, and my team of spirit guides who never let me fire them no matter how hard I tried.

All the mamas who've I had the pleasure of giving readings. I've learned from your spirit babies just as much as you have. I'm truly grateful.

My three boys, Finn, Roan, and Kai, for allowing me to leave for a week to write this book and for cleaning the kitty litter while I was gone. Oh, and for being the most amazing teachers I could have ever asked for.

WHAT ALL SPIRIT BABIES WANT THEIR MAMAS TO KNOW

And my husband and soulmate, Graeme. Thank you for your undying love and for being the one person who always totally gets me, even when I drive you crazy. I love you all 'da time. It's time for us to FLY.

Additional Resources from Kate Street and Love From Baby

Spirit Baby Videos:
How to Have Kick-Ass Prebirth Communication
The BEST Pregnancy Advice Ever
Getting Ready for Your Empowered Birth
Age and Pregnancy
Miscarriage
TTC (or Why the HELL is this taking so long?)
TTC or Being Pregnant After a Loss
The Healing of Your Traumatic Birth Experience
What Can I Do About This Unplanned Pregnancy?
Making Sense of Stillbirth all links for the above is:
http://lovefrombaby.com/get-a-pre-birth-reading/

Conscious Abortion
http://lovefrombaby.com/conscious-abortion/

Packages:
The TTC Game-Changer Package
http://lovefrombaby.com/the-ttc-package/

Miscarriage Package
http://lovefrombaby.com/miscarriage/

Pregnancy Package
http://lovefrombaby.com/the-pregnancy-package/

Opening Your Gift
Strengthen Your Natural Ability for Prebirth Communication.
http://lovefrombaby.com/opening-your-gift/

The Awakening Series
Working With the New Energy
Self-Love
Dark Night of The Soul
What the HELL is Going On With My Body?
Frequency Jumping
The Magic of a Limitless Life

http://lovefrombaby.com/awakening-series/

Meditation Download:
Messages from the Womb
Beautiful Birth

http://lovefrombaby.com/spirit-baby-meditation/

Free Articles and Videos:
Love From Baby Blog
http://lovefrombaby.com/blog/

Made in the USA
Lexington, KY
31 May 2017